I0528490

The Breathe Love Method

Harnessing the Power of Conscious Breathing for Mental Health and Wellness

Breathe Love !

Copyright © 2023

All Rights Reserved

ISBN:

Hardcover: 978-1-962381-22-2

Paperback: 978-1-962381-21-5

Dedication

To my mom, Georgia.

That altar call has been answered.

Acknowledgment

I would like to express my heartfelt gratitude to all those individuals whose unwavering support and guidance have propelled me forward. In particular, I am deeply thankful to Carol Lampman and Becky Beaton, who have been pillars of instruction and encouragement. I am indebted to David Yarborough for his invaluable advice that illuminated my path during challenging moments. The memory of the late John Bradshaw and his transformative workshop continues to resonate, offering profound healing to my grieving soul.

My sincere appreciation extends to all those who played a role in bringing this book to fruition, providing their unwavering assistance and encouragement. I am profoundly moved by the individuals who opened their hearts and souls in our breath circles, demonstrating the profound unity of existence through shared breath.

My journey as a musician has been enriched by the presence of remarkable souls who have shared their talents and spirits, particularly the SydPatrick Quartet and the Marching Southerners at Jacksonville State University.

To my soulmate, Stephanie, whose enduring love and loyalty have graced my life for over five decades, I am eternally thankful. My heartfelt gratitude also goes to my daughter Carrie and son-in-law Carl, who have steadfastly believed in me and contributed countless hours of their remarkable talents. And to my son David, whose luminous spirit shines brilliantly.

Lastly, I wish to acknowledge my guardian angel, Gabriella, whose presence has illuminated the beauty of pure love in its most exquisite form.

Contents

About the Author

Introducing W. Scott Ragsdale, Ph.D., LPC—an accomplished professional with an extensive range of credentials and a rich background. Possessing a Ph.D. in Theocentric Studies, he is a licensed professional counselor with adept skills in energy healing and psychotherapy. Beyond this, he serves as a spiritual mentor, breathwork practitioner, and meditation leader, adding a comprehensive element to his work. His expertise also encompasses roles as a Reiki Master, Qigong instructor, and practitioner of Heart Centered Hypnotherapy.

With a remarkable journey spanning sixty years, Dr. Ragsdale has taken on various roles, including those of a professional musician, educator, college psychology professor, and workshop presenter. What sets Dr. Ragsdale apart is the skillful integration of traditional psychotherapy with dynamic energy healing techniques such as Breath Work, Reiki, and Energy Psychology.

Throughout the past thirty years, his dedication has driven him to explore and delve into the realm of breath, resulting in the creation of a comprehensive pathway toward achieving holistic wellness.

Preface

In 1995, I began to hear a faint yet distinct voice that spoke of the union between Breath and Love. Little did I know that this realization would lead me on a journey of self-discovery and growth that was beyond my wildest dreams. My journey was one of triumphs and challenges, a journey of doubt, patience, frustration, and fear. Yet, it was also a journey of discovery, wonder, humility, joy, peace, vision, creativity, compassion, forgiveness, and, most importantly, Love.

Today, I know in my soul that consciously breathing Love is essential to a life of thriving, not just surviving. The experiences of my past and present have reaffirmed this conviction. The most significant affirmations have come from the changes in my personal life, my soul, and my faith, as well as the lives of those who have joined me in breathing love.

The Breathe Love Method does not aim to substitute any existing forms of prayer or expressions of love. Rather, it provides an extra source of empowerment for individuals desiring to profoundly and intimately encounter love within their hearts and souls.

By practicing breathing love as it has been taught and practiced through the ages, the practitioner will be led to a personal experience of unconditional Love, which is not always found in every loving experience.

The following chapters present compelling evidence from various sources that support the practice of breathing love. The evidence is rooted in biblical, spiritual, and historical contexts and supported by the practice and experience of saints and prophets from the Old and New Testament to the present.

Of particular significance is the fact that Jesus practiced and taught meditative prayer, which was His most common form of prayer. The history of the early Christian church and the saints who followed him also demonstrates how this form of meditative prayer has been discovered and rediscovered through the ages, reaffirming its importance.

The Breathe Love Method is not intended to be a new religion, ideology, theology, or doctrine. Rather, it is a practice that is compatible with all religions that believe in the power of God's Love. While supporting evidence is important, the true affirmation of the power of breathing love comes from practice and experience. This principle is consistently found in the writings of those who practice meditative prayer, from Jesus to the present.

To experience the power of breathing love for yourself, consider attending the Breathe Love Method Workshop or using the workbook that accompanies this book. By practicing breathing love, you can experience love in your heart and know the Truth that will set you free.

It is worth noting that while 70% of Americans claim they want to grow spiritually, only 19% have had a powerful spiritual experience. This discrepancy may be due to the fact that many Americans rely on verbal prayer, which may not be as effective as meditation and the practice of breathing love. Therefore, to improve one's spirituality, it is essential to embrace breathing, Love, and meditation in a way that Western cultures have not emphasized.

This book is the culmination of my journey and the deep, abiding experience of Love that comes from the practice of breathing love. From the outset, it is essential to state that breathing love is not the only way to experience Love, nor is there a one-size-fits-all approach to experiencing Love. The methods and manners of experiencing Love are unlimited and varied, a testament to the power of creation.

Page Blank Intentionally

Chapter 1: Introduction to Conscious Breathing and Love Energy

Breathing is the key to our existence, yet it often goes unnoticed in our daily lives. Doesn't it? Until you feel that there is something off with how you are feeling. The way you naturally breathe can have a significant impact on your physical and mental health. Research has shown that your breathing patterns can shift based on your emotions and thoughts. For example, when you feel happy, you tend to take slow, deep breaths. This leads to the release of hormones such as endorphins, dopamine, oxytocin, and serotonin that promote happiness. Conversely, when you experience anger or stress, you may take short, rapid breaths. This activates stress receptors in the amygdala region, an almond-shaped structure in the brain that is primarily responsible for processing emotions, particularly fear and anxiety. It plays a critical role in the body's flight or flight response triggering the release of hormones such as adrenaline and cortisol in response to perceived threats. By becoming more aware of your breathing and intentionally adjusting your breathing patterns, you can help regulate your emotions and improve your overall well-being.

When you feel your breaths are shallow and rapid,

perchance, you may intentionally harness them to slow and deep. Henceforth as the name suggests, conscious breathing aims to bring awareness to your Breath and deliberately alter your breathing pattern for a specific purpose. This can include a range of health-related benefits, whether physical, mental, or emotional. To practice conscious breathing, you need to focus on your Breath and consciously control its rhythm and depth as it enters and leaves your body. This means paying attention to the physical sensations of the Breath, such as the feeling of air moving into your nose and leaving your body through your mouth as you feel the air on your lips or the rise and fall of your chest or belly. By focusing on your Breath, you can bring your mind into the present moment and reduce distracting thoughts and feelings.

You can also activate the body's relaxation response or the sympathetic nervous system, depending on the type of breathing technique used and the desired result required. For example, now that you know that slow, deep breathing can activate the relaxation response, you can practice deep breathing exercises to achieve serenity and relax the tensed muscles. On the other hand, while in some situations, activating the sympathetic system can be beneficial, such as in emergency situations that require quick action or in sports or other activities that require a burst of energy and heightened physical performance, you can have a short-term activation of the sympathetic system that can improve cognitive function and increase focus and alertness.

By now, you've likely come across the concept of conscious breathing. In a world that seems to move faster every day, it's no wonder that stress and anxiety-reducing techniques are often discussed. Breathing practices are among the most popular and effective ways to combat these issues. However, have you ever thought about using your breathing to help you feel more Love and kindness toward yourself and others? Are you familiar with the concept of Breathing Love that allows you to fill yourself with Love to have a fulfilling life and connect with God and become one with Love. If not, let me walk you through the path of Breathing Love and feeling God every time you breathe to establish a personal connection with God by experiencing the presence of the Divine Breath.

The Spirit of God(Love) has been present on this earth ever since the creation of this world. In Genesis, chapter 1, verse 2 says, "the Spirit of God(Love) is described as hovering over the waters" before the creation of the world. The Hebrew Word for "Spirit" is "ruach," which can also be translated as "breath" or "wind." This suggests that the Spirit of God(Love) is intimately connected to the act of breathing and the movement of air.

Then, God created light and separated it from the darkness, bringing order to chaos. And as God created the heavens and the earth, God breathed life into all living creatures. This Breath, also known as the Breath of God(Love), is what gives life to all things. As you take in each Breath, you are reminded of the presence of the Divine within you, and therefore, you can connect with the Spirit of God(Love) that hovers over you, giving you life and guiding you on your journey.

Now that you know that the Spirit of God is the Breath of God, you must also know that Bible teaches that God is

Love. This means that Love is not just something that God does, but it is an essential part of who God is. The Apostle John writes in 1 John 4:8, "Whoever does not love does not know God, because God is love." When you consider the connection between the Spirit of God and Breath and the fact that God is Love, it is natural to think of the Breath of God as the Breath of Love. In other words, the Spirit of God is the manifestation of God's Love in the world, and it is through the Breath of God that you can experience and connect with this Love.

Breathing can also be seen as a metaphor for the flow of Love in your life. Just as the Breath flows in and out of your body, the Love of God can flow into you and out of you, connecting you with God and with others. Conscious breathing practices, such as "breathing love," can be a way to intentionally connect with the Breath of Love and experience a deeper sense of connection and unity with God and with others.

Moreover, the practice of Breathing Love is not limited to any particular religion or belief system. It is a universal practice that is accessible to anyone seeking a personal connection with the divine through the experience of the Spirit of God. The Breath of God, also known as "Manna," "Chi," "Holy Spirit," "Light," "Fire," or "Karma," is a manifestation of divine energy that can be experienced through conscious breathing. Interestingly, in ancient Aramaic, Hebrew, and Greek languages, the words "word," "breath," and "spirit" share the same root meaning. This suggests that reading ancient religious texts with this understanding can reveal a deeper mystical message that the Spirit of God is the Breath of God and that God's essence is

Love, which can be experienced through the practice of Breathing Love.

In many traditions, the Breath is seen as the source of life and vitality, and breath practices are deemed as a means to reconnect to the source of life. It is the essence of your being, connecting you to the world around you and to the divine. Not just in the Judeo-Christian tradition does the Breath of God represents the divine spark to experience Love, but breath practices have a long history in various Eastern mystical, Buddhist, Hindu, and Islamic traditions, dating back thousands of years. These practices have been used as a means to attain spiritual enlightenment, a deeper level of awareness to promote physical and mental well-being, and to connect with the divine.

Meditative prayer, in its various forms, is a common practice across many of the world's religions, including Buddhism, Hinduism, Judaism, Christianity, and Islam, as well as in primal and tribal religions. In all of these traditions, the importance of the Breath in meditative prayer is universally recognized, either directly or indirectly.

In Buddhist traditions, breath practices are a fundamental part of meditation, with a focus on developing mindfulness and awareness of one's Spirit. The Buddha himself taught the Anapanasati Sutta, a discourse on mindfulness of breathing, as a means to cultivate mental concentration and overcome negative mental states. Similarly, in Hinduism, the concept of Prana, the vital life force that pervades the universe, is closely tied to breath practices. Yogic breathing, or Pranayama, is used to control the flow of Prana within the body and to achieve a state of balance and harmony. Also, in

Islamic traditions, the practice of Dhikr involves the repetition of the name of Allah, often combined with deep breathing and rhythmic movement. This practice is intended to cultivate a deep sense of remembrance and awareness that each Breath you consciously inhale is a means of taking in Love.

For centuries, spiritual mystics have emphasized the importance of achieving a personal connection with God through meditative prayer accompanied by controlled breathing. It is widely believed that every Breath we take contains a powerful energy of Love, as has been expressed by mystics throughout history. Despite the religious origins of these practices, they can be used by anyone, regardless of their religious beliefs, because everyone and everything centers around one Breath and one Love. They are not exclusive to any particular religion and can be used by anyone seeking to improve their physical, mental, and spiritual well-being.

Over time, in Western religions, there has been a tendency to overlook the everyday practice of meditative breathing. Instead, this practice has been restricted to secluded communities and the ministry, leading to a lack of emphasis on its importance for the wider community. While meditative breathing has been a staple of Eastern spiritual practices for thousands of years, it has been largely ignored or downplayed in Western religions. This is a shame, as meditative breathing is a powerful tool for connecting with the divine and experiencing spiritual growth.

On the contrary, these Western religions have placed a greater emphasis on verbal prayer and ritualistic practices rather than on cultivating a personal connection with the divine through Breathing Love. This has led to a lack of understanding and appreciation for the benefits of inhaling God's Breath to enjoy the unlimited benefits it offers not only among the community members but also their leaders.

It is essential to keep in mind that this book may not be suitable for everyone. Out of 210 million Americans who identify as Christian, around 100 million are evangelical Christians. While this book's teachings are rooted in biblical and spiritual evidence, they might not align with the beliefs and practices of some in the evangelical community.

As an evangelical Christian, you should be aware that this book may not be in line with your religious beliefs, and neither do I intend to impose this on you. You are free to put this book down and not open it ever again because you never were my intended reader. But if you are seeking to establish a personal connection with God and want to experience the divine Breath in your everyday lives, then this piece of work is specifically written for you. If you are looking for a more meaningful spiritual experience beyond traditional prayer practices, then this book is for you.

Chapter 2: Love Energy in the Bible

While the Bible does not explicitly refer to Breath as "love energy," it does contain teachings and passages that connect the concepts of Breath and Love. The Bible portrays Love not only as a central attribute of God and encourages us to love one another but also tells us that it is the very nature of God. There are several instances in the Bible where God's Love is demonstrated through God's actions, and hence those actions are said to be perceived to be God's Love for us. Similarly, Breath itself is not equated to love energy directly, yet there are biblical ideas that emphasize the connection between Breath and Love.

Breath is the source of life and the essence of every living being that carries significant theological and spiritual implications. Throughout the Bible, Breath is consistently portrayed as a vital aspect of human existence, intimately linked to God's creative power and the very essence of life itself. One must also beware that where Breath is the source of life, God is the source of that Breath. Genesis 2:7 is the most explicit and foundational example of this. Moreover, in Ezekiel 37, the prophet is shown a vision of dry bones, symbolizing spiritual desolation. As Ezekiel prophesies, the Breath of God enters the bones, bringing them back to life and representing spiritual restoration and renewal.

We also learned in the previous chapter that God is Love, and it is reasonable to associate God'sBreath with the Breath of Love. In the Bible, God's Breath is often associated with life-giving power and presence. If God's essence is Love, then God's Breath can be seen as an expression of that Love, as it is intimately linked to God'svery nature.

When considering the connection between Breath and Love, you can draw a parallel between the life-giving Breath of God and the outpouring of Love from the heart. Just as Breath sustains physical life, Love has the power to bring life, healing, and restoration of oneself and to relationships and communities. Both Breath and Love are essential for the well-being and flourishing of individuals and communities.

Even though many Bible translations do not directly equate Breath to love energy, the teachings on Love and the imagery of Breath are intertwined in a metaphorical sense. The Breath we receive from God can be seen as a symbol of God's Love and presence within us, animating and empowering us to love one another. By imparting God's Breath, God not only brings physical life to humanity but also infuses it with God's divine Love and purpose. This Breath of life, when outpouring into us, becomes a reflection of God's Love, and therefore, when we breathe more and more of God's Love, we end up being like God and loving others.

The Apostle Paul, in his letter to Romans 5:5, writes about the Love of God being poured into our hearts through the Holy Spirit (Ruach). Here, the Breath of God, represented by the Holy Spirit, is associated with the outpouring of God's Love within us. Furthermore, the association between Breath and the Holy Spirit in the Bible strengthens the connection between God's Breath and Love. The Holy Spirit is often symbolically represented as a Breath or wind. In the New Testament, the Holy Spirit is described as the presence of God dwelling within us, guiding and empowering us to live in loving kindness. This indicates that when the Spirit of God starts to dwell in us, we become one. 1 Corinthians 6:17: Paul declares that the one who is joined with God is one with God's Breath. This statement emphasizes the unity and inseparable bond between us and God through the Holy Spirit. It implies that through our union with the Holy Spirit, we become partakers of the divine nature and experience a deep spiritual oneness with God's Love.

So, while the Bible does not explicitly use the phrase "the breath of love," the understanding that God is Love and that God's Breath represents God's life-giving power and presence allows us to make the connection between God's Breath and the Breath of Love. It highlights the intimate relationship between God's essence, God's Breath, and the expression of Love in the world. Now, for example, take a look at this passage from the book of Job 34:14-15, which states

if the Spirit and Breath of God were to be withdrawn, all humanity would perish together, and mankind would return to dust.

There is no doubt that if God's Spirit and His Love were taken away from us, there would be nothing left of us. Thus God summarized the entire law and Torah in two commandments which were both based on Love. Perhaps one reason why God is connected with us through the source of life (Breath) is to remind ourselves with each inhale and exhale that our purpose on this earth is to live our lives filled with Love energy.

The idea of love energy can be seen as a way to understand the power of Love in our lives, inspired by the Holy Breath. It draws upon the notion that just as we need Breath to live, we also need Love for our well-being. We can metaphorically compare the life-giving nature of Breath to the nurturing and transformative power of Love. Just as we inhale Breath to sustain our physical life, we can recognize that with each breath we take, we can also receive and experience Love and healing that God provides. This perspective reminds us that Love is essential for us to live a fulfilling and meaningful life. It emphasizes that through every Breath we take, we have the opportunity to receive the Love and healing that we need to thrive.

Additionally, Saint Scholastica, a Christian saint who lived in the 6th century, emphasized that we receive spiritual guidance with each Breath we take. This concept implies that there is a deeper connection between our Breath and our spiritual journey that draws us even closer to God. I would say that her suggestion is applicable not only in the Christian context but in many spiritual traditions since Breath is regarded as more than just a physical act. In various other religions, it is seen as a vehicle for connecting with the divine or accessing higher realms of consciousness because by focusing on our Breath and being mindful of its rhythm and flow, we can cultivate a sense of presence and openness to receive spiritual guidance.

There are instances in the Bible indicating that Breath directly connects us to the Spirit of God. Such as:

1. **In John 20:22,** it is recorded that Jesus appeared to His disciples and breathed on them, saying, "Receive the Holy Spirit." This event holds profound spiritual significance when you substitute "Breath" for "Spirit."

   By breathing on His disciples, Jesus imparted the Holy Breath to them. This act represented the initiation of a new spiritual era for the disciples. The Breath of Jesus can be seen as a representation of divine life-giving power. It signified the transfer of His own spiritual essence to empower and equip the disciples for their future ministry.

2. In his book "Rabbi Jesus," Bruce Chilton explores the teachings and practices of Jesus in the context of the Jewish traditions of his time. Chilton suggests that Jesus learned about the principles of the Spirit of God in our Breath through John the Baptist, who in turn taught the teachings and prayer practices of the prophet Ezekiel.

   Ezekiel had experiences and visions that involved the Spirit of God. In Ezekiel 37:1-14, there is a powerful vision of the valley of dry bones, where the prophet sees a vast multitude of bones coming to life as the Breath of God enters them. This vision symbolizes the restoration and revitalization of Israel through the power of God's Breath.

   Similarly, when people receive the Spirit of God, they are healed and start life anew. Their souls and bodies are now breathing God's Love and are beginning to rejuvenate.

With a breath of God comes several benefits and advantages. Without God's Breath, our spirits are barely alive; they are like people on ventilation who are alive just enough not to be declared dead but shallow on the inside. Therefore, when God breathes, Holy Love enters our body and brings healing. As a result, we begin to experience peace and comfort. And not just comfort and healing, God's Love also enlightens us with divine Truth and understanding. Discussed below are a number of benefits that walk into our lives as we receive God's Love.

1. **God's Breath comforts and heals:** In 2 Samuel 22:16-20, David describes God's intervention in response to his distress. He speaks metaphorically of God's Breath as a powerful force that parts the heavens, revealing God's presence and descending to rescue him. This imagery suggests that God's Breath symbolizes divine intervention, bringing comfort and salvation.

2. **The Breath of God gives understanding:** Job 32:8, *"But it is the spirit in a person, the breath of the Almighty, that gives them understanding,"* states that the Spirit or Breath of God gives understanding to a person. This verse suggests that the Breath of God is the source of wisdom and insight that surpasses human understanding. It signifies a spiritual enlightenment that brings clarity and discernment, emphasizing the importance of recognizing God's presence and guidance in attaining true understanding. This couldn't be more true because

we can actually see this happening on various occasions in the Bible.

3. **Lies, worry, fear, and pain is taken away with the Breath:** Isaiah 57:11. The passage highlights how the people's lies, worry, fear, and pain stems from their separation from God's Love and that these things can merely be blown away with a breath. *"the wind will carry all of them off, a mere breath will blow them away.*

4. **Every man is devoid of knowledge (Truth) without the Breath of God:** Jeremiah 10:14-15 tells us that the Breath of God, which is the Holy Spirit, is the source of divine knowledge, wisdom, and Truth. Without the guidance of the Holy Spirit, humans are incapable of understanding the Truth.

The Breath of God/ Spirit of God is not only capable of these gentle and tender works, but it also has the immense capacity to bring a whirlwind, shake the mountains, and much more. The idea that the Breath (Spirit) is directly connected to the unlimited power of Love stems from the understanding that Love is the ultimate source of life and sustainer of all creation. There are several instances where we see God's unlimited power with divine Breath/Spirit demonstrating its capacity and the wonders Love can do.

The book of Psalms, in chapter 18, verse 15, states, *"Then the channels of the sea were seen, and the foundations of the world were laid bare at your rebuke, O Lord, at the blast of the breath of your nostrils."* The mention of the blast of the Breath from God's nostrils emphasizes the magnitude and power of this display through the work of Love in creation.

In Exodus 15:8, a blast from God's Breath parts the waters. (New Living Bible) This story is spiritually significant when we understand that "water" in ancient languages metaphorically represents our emotions.

Moreover, there are various gifts of the Holy Spirit that demonstrate the unlimited power of Love. These are found in the first letter to the Corinthians in its 12th chapter:

1. The Gift of Wisdom, as discussed even in point 2 previously.
2. The Gift of Knowledge.
3. The Gift of Faith.
4. The Gift of Healing.
5. The Gift of Miracles.
6. The Gift of Prophecy.
7. The Gift of Discerning Spirits.

Since we depend on the Breath/Spirit of God, we must understand and accept its profound significance in every aspect of human existence. We have explored various biblical references and witnessed how the Breath/Spirit of God serves as the very source of life and the essence of all living beings. It's the undeniable intimate connection to the Love of God, as evidenced by the powerful act of Jesus breathing upon His disciples, imparting the Holy Spirit. The teachings of John the Baptist and the awe-inspiring account of Ezekiel breathing life into dry bones further exemplify the transformative nature of the Breath.

Moreover, the Breath/Spirit of God is not merely a life force but a gateway to comfort, healing, divine Truth, and understanding. Lies, worry, fear, and pain swiftly eradicates in the presence of the Breath. By embracing this divine connection, we open ourselves up to the limitless power of Love, capable of shaking nations and surging forth like an unstoppable torrent. It is through the nurturing and cherishing of our Breath that we unlock the boundless wisdom and experience profound spiritual growth, forever aligning ourselves with the undeniable presence of Love energy. Thus, let us embrace the irrefutable truth that the Breath/Spirit of God is not only vital but also indispensable in our journey toward a life of purpose, fulfillment, and inner peace.

Chapter 3: Breathing Love and Prayer

Let there remain just great silence before God,

the silence that becomes prayer.

— Pope John Paul II

Prayer is a remarkable practice that transcends boundaries and unites people from all walks of life, regardless of their religious or cultural background. It is a powerful tool for self-reflection, connection, and finding solace in something greater than ourselves. So, whether you identify as a follower of a specific faith or simply seek a deeper connection with the divine, prayer offers a universal path that is open to everyone. The ways in which people pray are as diverse as the individuals themselves, and every approach is equally valid. According to Smith (1961), the world's religions share more similarities than differences, and this holds true for the concept of prayer as well.

When you explore the diverse tapestry of humanity, you will discover that prayer is deeply ingrained in the fabric of countless religions and cultures. It is a thread that weaves through the rich tapestry of your collective spiritual journey. From Christianity to Islam, Hinduism to Buddhism, and Judaism to indigenous practices, prayer finds its rightful place in each of these belief systems. Its essence is not confined to a specific set of rituals or words, but rather, it is the intent, the yearning, and the surrender that make prayer a universal language of the soul.

It's important to note that this discussion on prayer is not meant to compare or belittle any specific method of prayer. Instead, the purpose of this chapter is to offer a broad reflection on the universally accepted principles and methods of prayer, demonstrating how it can be combined with Breath to create an immediate and powerful process for connecting with and accepting the universal God/Christ spirit.

Beyond the rituals and external expressions, prayer serves as a vehicle for connection, both within ourselves and with a higher power. It is a sacred space where you can pour out your hopes, fears, gratitude, and aspirations, knowing that you are heard and understood. Through prayer, you acknowledge your vulnerabilities, seek guidance, and express your deepest longings. It becomes a sanctuary where you can find solace, healing, and a renewed sense of purpose. No matter your background or the specifics of your beliefs, prayer invites you to explore your inner landscape and cultivate a profound connection with something beyond the confines of the material world. It offers a pathway to self-discovery, spiritual growth, and a deeper understanding of the universal truths that bind us all.

The essence of prayer can be found in its Latin roots, where *"precarious"* signifies obtaining through begging, and *"precarious"* denotes earnest entreaty and imploring. These meanings convey the core idea that prayer is a heartfelt plea, a sincere request that goes beyond mere words. Two common forms of prayer are:

1. **The petition,** a common form of prayer, involves making specific requests to a higher power. It is an act of expressing your needs, desires, and hopes, recognizing that you are dependent on divine intervention. Throughout history, numerous biblical passages illustrate the practice of petitionary prayer, showcasing the significance of this form of communication with the divine.

    In the book of Matthew 7:7-8, Jesus encourages his disciples, saying, *"Ask and it will be given to you; seek, and you will find; knock and the door will be opened to you. For everyone who asks receives; the one who seeks finds; and to the one who knocks, the door will be opened."* These verses emphasize the power of asking and seeking in prayer, assuring believers that our petitions will be heard and answered.

2. **Intercession**, another significant form of prayer, entails pleading on behalf of others and seeking divine intervention in their lives. It is an act of compassion, demonstrating your willingness to intercede for the needs, well-being, and spiritual growth of others. The practice of intercession is found throughout the Bible, where various individuals intercede for their communities, loved ones, and even enemies.

    One notable example of intercession is found in the book of Exodus. In Exodus 32:11-14, Moses fervently intercedes for the people of Israel after they worshiped a golden calf, pleading for God's mercy and forgiveness. Moses pleads, *"Turn from your fierce anger; relent and do not bring disaster on your people. Remember your servants Abraham, Isaac, and Israel, to whom you swore by your own self: 'I will make your descendants as numerous as the stars in the sky, and I will give your descendants all this land I promised them, and it will be their inheritance forever.'"* Moses' intercession demonstrates his deep concern for the people and willingness to stand in the gap, appealing to God's promises and mercy.

In his work, Foster (1982) explores twenty-one distinct categories of prayer, highlighting the vast array of ways in which you can engage in this sacred practice. Ulanov (1982) goes even further, proclaiming prayer as the most fundamental and primal form of human speech. It surpasses the constraints of language, manifesting as sighs, gestures, or even profound silence, as expressed by Dossey (1993).

This explains that prayer is a versatile and multifaceted phenomenon that can take various forms, be it in the context of expression or practice, which can occur in different contexts. Since it is a deeply personal and individual experience, allowing each person to connect with the divine in their unique way, you may opt for various contexts depending on your preference. You may realize through the following list which one of these befits you or has been your practice ever since you began to connect with God through the Spirit. However, it is important to note that each of these contexts has its own significance.

1. **Individual prayer:** When engaging in individual prayer, you have the freedom to express your innermost thoughts, desires, and gratitude to a higher power, fostering a direct and intimate connection.

2. **Communal endeavor:** On the other hand, prayer can also be a communal endeavor, where individuals come together in shared devotion, unity, and support. Participating in group prayer allows for a sense of collective spiritual energy as people join their voices, intentions, and faith, creating a powerful and uplifting experience.

3. **Private act:** Furthermore, prayer can be conducted in the solitude of your own sacred space. It provides an opportunity for deep introspection, reflection, and communion with the divine, away from external distractions. Private prayer allows you to express your innermost emotions, seek guidance, and find solace in a deeply personal way.

4. **Public expression:** At times, prayer can be a public expression of faith, where individuals come together in religious services, ceremonies, or public gatherings. Public prayer allows for the proclamation of shared beliefs, the reinforcement of community values, and the demonstration of devotion in a more visible and communal manner.

Moreover, prayer is not limited to conscious awareness. It can arise from the depths of your unconscious mind, emerging in ways you may not even realize. It can come in the form of dreams, where your subconscious communicates with the divine, bypassing your waking awareness. These dream encounters with the divine can offer insights, messages, and spiritual experiences that may deeply impact and guide your life.

Just as prayer transcends the boundaries of context and expression, it is also crucial for you to be aware of the fact that prayer holds a profound spiritual dimension that extends beyond the boundaries of time, space, and matter. It is a remarkable nonlocal event, transcending the limitations of the present moment. This suggests that within you lies a part of your psyche that is also nonlocal and infinite. In the Western tradition, this infinite aspect of your psyche is often referred to as the Spirit. The ability to engage in prayer, which is the act of connecting with the divine through mental action, unveils significant spiritual implications, such as your inherent capacity to tap into the nonlocal qualities of the Divine, the God/Christ within you. This Divine essence is infinite, omnipresent, and eternal.

Moreover, empirical evidence further supports the power of prayer, emphasizing its connection to the nonlocal aspects of the Divine. This evidence highlights the profound impact that prayer can have on your lives, reaching beyond the confines of physicality and touching the depths of your Spirit.

Recognizing the nonlocal nature of prayer and its alignment with the infinite qualities of the Divine enables you to receive the presence of God and enter the nonphysical realm opening up vast possibilities for your spiritual growth and transformation. It invites you to embrace prayer as a means to tap into your true essence, connecting with the infinite and eternal aspects of your being. This realization empowers you on your spiritual journey, reminding you of the profound depths that lie within your souls and the limitless connection you have with the divine presence. Prayer enables you to transcend the physical realm and enter a nonphysical realm closer to the Divine power. This connection not only shifts your awareness but also strengthens the relationship between you and Love energy. Since you are closer to God and both reside in the same realm, you can expect love energy to touch you more deeply than in the physical (mind/body) world. This proves why people engage in prayer and feel more connected to God and are able to understand the mysteries of the nonphysical and spiritual realms because they have been made aware of them through the strengthening of their connection with God, along with establishing a love relationship.

For a long time, Western religious ideas have portrayed God as separate from humanity, residing high above us. In this perspective, prayers are sent upwards to God, who then decides whether or not to respond. However, Joseph Campbell refers to this external perception of God as a unique and problematic belief found mainly in Western culture, not shared by most other world religions. While this notion brings comfort to many, those who advocate for preserving this view of prayer may inadvertently hinder its growth and evolution, preventing it from adapting and remaining relevant (Dossey, 1993). On the other hand, Holmes (1938) emphasizes that prayer is crucial for the happiness and conscious well-being of the soul.

It is fascinating to recognize that prayer not only serves as a powerful tool for establishing a loving relationship with the universal God/Christ that promotes your well-being but also guides you on a transformative journey of becoming effective lovers of the Divine (Foster, 1992). Prayer opens the doors of your hearts and minds, allowing the Love between you and the universal God/Christ to flow freely. Within the sacred space of prayer, you express your Love, seek guidance, and deepen your connection with the divine presence. It is through this nurturing relationship cultivated by prayer that your capacity to embody and share Love expands, extending its transformative power to the world around you.

While definitions, terminology, and conversations about prayer hold significance, they do not change the core reality that prayer is fundamentally a relationship of love with the universal God/Christ. The language of enduring, continuous, and growing Love becomes the very essence of prayer. This love relationship calls for a reciprocal response, as real prayer is about becoming effective lovers and falling deeply in Love with the universal God/Christ spirit.

Everyone prays in their own language,
and there is no language that God does not understand.
Duke Ellington

It is crucial to realize that because you invest yourself in prayer, you might end up assuming that you are the leader in this relationship and that you might begin to want all of these benefits and prosperities according to your own way. However, the truth is that prayer is an answer and blessing in itself, and it cannot be confined to rigid notions or fixed ideas. When you try to confine prayer within fixed boundaries, you limit the immense power of the universal God/Christ, which is the source of your prayers and the essence of your Spirit. Remember that even being able to initiate prayer and engage in it on a daily basis, you need assistance from God, as highlighted in Romans 8:26; *in the same way, the Spirit helps us in our weakness. We do not know what we ought to pray for, but the Spirit himself intercedes for us through wordless groans.*

Therefore instead of growing impulsive about the outcomes, just cheer on the fact that prayer is the key that unlocks the depths of your being, fostering a mutual exchange of Love and grace between you and the universal God/Christ. In this journey of Love through prayer, you discover a sense of fulfillment, spiritual growth, and a radiant expression of Love that radiates into every aspect of your life. As you engage in prayer, embrace this sacred practice with an open heart and mind, knowing that you are tapping into a realm that surpasses the boundaries of the physical world and brings you closer and closer to the Divine energy. Allow prayer to nourish your soul, deepen your love connection with the Divine, and awaken the infinite potential within you.

METHODS OF PRAYER

The longing to pray appears to be ingrained within all human beings, as evidenced by its presence throughout history. Despite attempts, including torture and war, to impose a "correct" way of praying, people have resisted and remained true to their individual experiences. Since there is no "correct" way to pray, the following methods are offered to facilitate a greater connection to the heart of the universal God/ Christ and should be accepted or discarded based on individual experience.

The Spindrift Studies stand out as one of the most

renowned long-term investigations into prayer. Notably, these studies have shed light on the comparison between directed and non-directed prayer (Dossey, 1994).

1. **Directed prayer:** This form of prayer refers to a specific form of prayer where there is a particular goal, intention, or desired outcome in mind. It involves consciously directing one's thoughts, words, and intentions toward a specific request or purpose. In direct prayer, there is a sense of actively seeking something from the divine, often expressed through specific prayers or supplications.

2. **Non-directed prayer:** This is an open-ended form of prayer that does not have a specific goal or outcome in mind. It is a prayer practice characterized by surrendering and allowing oneself to be receptive to whatever arises in the prayer experience. Non-directed prayer involves being present at the moment, connecting with the divine, and being open to the guidance, insights, and blessings that may unfold naturally during the prayer.

The Spindrift Studies provide us with valuable insights, showing that both methods of prayer have been experimentally proven to have effects beyond chance. However, the outcomes reveal a compelling fact: Non-directed prayer is consistently two to four times more effective than directed prayer. This suggests that while it is important to acknowledge the value of directed prayer, incorporating phrases like "Thy Will be done" or "Your Highest Good" can greatly enhance your spiritual empowerment.

Surrendering yourself becomes a significant element in non-directed prayer. By letting go of your personal desires and intentions, you create space for a deeper connection with the divine. Through surrender, you align your own will with the divine will, placing your trust in the unfolding of the highest good in your life. Embracing surrender in your prayers leads to profound spiritual growth and transformation. In the exploration of prayer, Quinn (1992) discovered that surrender plays a significant role in the success of Therapeutic Touch. It's important to note that surrendering is distinct from simply "giving up." Surrender is an active and empowering choice that continuously empowers the Spirit, unlike the disempowering choice of inaction associated with giving up (Dossey, 1994). In non-directed prayer, the objective is not to empty the mind or lack direction but rather to surrender to whatever images, goals, or outcomes arise during prayer. This surrender becomes an integral aspect of connecting with God in prayer.

According to Kelsey (1976), non-directed prayer emphasizes the profound experience of being in the presence of God. It places greater importance on our encounter with God rather than solely focusing on what we desire from God (intentional prayer). When you pray in this manner, you often receive blessings beyond what you could have dared to ask for on your own. Jesus himself taught his disciples to pray in this way through the Lord's Prayer, highlighting the significance of surrendering and being in the presence of God.

Other biblical principles concerning prayer that are a part of The Breath Love Method are:

1. **To Pray Continuously:** The references 1 Timothy 3:10, 1 Timothy 5:7, and Luke 18:1 emphasize the importance of praying continuously. This means maintaining an ongoing and consistent connection with God throughout your lives, offering prayers day and night without ceasing. The Breathe Love Method allows you to pray without ceasing with conscious breathing, bringing awareness to the love energy within you.

2. **To Pray in Solitude:** Matthew 6:6 and Luke 5:16 highlight the significance of finding solitude for prayer. These verses encourage you to retreat to a quiet and inner space, away from distractions, to commune with God and seek His presence.

3. **To Pray with Your Heart and Soul:** 1 Corinthians 11:4 and Acts 1:4 emphasize that genuine prayer involves engaging your whole being, not just your intellect. Praying with sincerity and authenticity, allowing your heart and soul to be fully present, enables a deeper connection with God.

4. **To Pray in a Spirit of Faith and Surrender:** Luke 22:32 and Acts 10:22 teach you about the importance of approaching prayer with faith and surrender. Having faith in God's power and trusting in His will, you can surrender your own desires and submit to His divine guidance.

5. **Prayer Leads to Healing and Courage:** Luke 21:36 and James 5:16 reveal that prayer is a source of strength, healing, and courage. Additionally, research indicates that healing prayer can involve the transmission of healing energy or the presence of the

divine Spirit from one person or group to another (Weston, 1998). According to Kelsey (1976), a key aspect of Christianity and spirituality is recognizing that God actively seeks you and desires a relationship with you. Through prayer, you can find inner strength, seek intercession for healing, and support one another in times of need.

In conclusion, the principles of prayer offer you a path to experience the inner presence of God. Jeanne Guyon, a spiritualist of the Seventeenth Century, emphasized the importance of practices such as silence, solitude, praying the Bible, continuous prayer, and surrendering your ego to God as ways to encounter the divine within us. Despite facing persecution and execution for her beliefs, Guyon remained steadfast in her conviction that the universal Love of God resides within each of us, accessible at any time. It is important to acknowledge that following this spiritual path of prayer may encounter skepticism and criticism from those who have not yet experienced a deep personal connection with God's Love beyond traditional religious activities. However, it is crucial not to abandon other ways of experiencing God but rather to embrace the discovery of God within us, which enhances our awareness and acceptance of the divine in all aspects of life. Breathing Love, a continuous non-directed prayer method based on biblical principles, invites you to engage in guided non-directed prayer, prioritizing being in the presence of God over specific intentions or intercessions. Through the practice of the Breathe Love Method, you open yourself to receiving divine blessings far beyond what you could ask or expect. May the Breath Love Method be a transformative journey that deepens our connection with the Love of God and leads you to a life filled with Love, Truth, courage, and healing.

Chapter 4: Techniques for Conscious Breathing

In the realm of conscious breathing, various techniques have emerged as valuable tools to promote relaxation, enhance focus, and foster a profound sense of inner calm. Breathing is a fundamental and instinctual process that sustains your life, but it also holds immense potential for transforming your well-being on a deeper level. Through the act of recognizing your breath and actively connecting with it, you can access a potent instrument for uncovering more about yourself, achieving a state of relaxation, and fostering personal development. Throughout history, various cultures and traditions have recognized the profound benefits of conscious breathing practices, incorporating them into their everyday lives and healing modalities. In this chapter, you will explore a range of techniques that harness the power of conscious breathing, promoting various energies in your life, such as Love, peace, safety, and Truth. It is important to note that in the Breath Love Method, different exercises are aimed at attracting different powers and healings in your life.

Connected Breath/ Circular Breath

Circular breathing, also known as connected breathing, is the best way to start. It is an ancient practice where inhalation and exhalation are seamlessly connected without any pauses between   Figure1 them. It involves a continuous and smooth flow of breath, creating a circular pattern of breathing. (See Figure 1).

This method is frequently employed in activities such as meditation, breathwork, and specific musical instruments to ensure an ongoing stream of air and uphold a steady tempo. Proficiency in circular breathing enables you to encounter an unbroken breath cycle, fostering feelings of relaxation, concentration, and an enhanced state of mindfulness. Connected breathing is performed with the mouth open, creating a continuous flow of breath. *"I opened my mouth wide and panted, For I longed for Thy commandments"* *Psalm 119:13.*

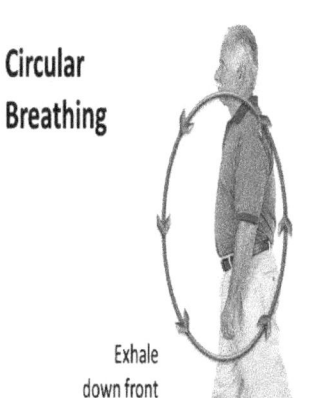

Circular Breathing

Exhale down front

Inhale up back

1. As you engage in connected breathing, envision your breath moving in a circular motion.
2. Initiate the breath from the pelvis, drawing the air up your back and into your throat.
3. Upon exhaling, allow the breath to descend without interruption, creating a circle down the front of your body back to the pelvis.
4. Each breath seamlessly transitions into the next, without pauses in between.
5. Visualize the breath encompassing the entirety of your inhalation and exhalation, rounding out both the top and bottom of the breath.

6. Maintain a smooth and rhythmic pattern of breathing throughout the practice.

To optimize the benefits of Breathing Love (Spirit of God), maintain a slow and deep breathing tempo, allowing more air to enter than during your usual resting breath. When exhaling, ensure a complete state of relaxation without any force or haste. Let the exhale occur naturally, effortlessly "falling out." Moreover, as you engage in this circular breathing technique, silently recite non-directed phrases with each inhale and exhale. On the inhale, focus on the phrase *"I am,"* and on the exhale, center your attention on the phrase *"At Peace."*

It would be great if you allocate 15-20 minutes each day to practice this method of circular breathing. Find a quiet and tranquil space where you can either sit or lie on your back. Through consistent daily practice, you will experience a stilling of the mind and body, and your awareness of the immediate presence of Love energy will expand.

You might be surprised to know that these repeated experiences of breathing love are rooted throughout centuries in various religious traditions. They have been recognized as a pathway to establishing a personal relationship built on trust and, eventually, experiencing the transformative power of Love in its entirety. The mystics and saints who have delved into the practice of meditative breathing have consistently emphasized the importance of continuous meditation.

Placing trust in the power of your breath, you can effectively reverse the patterns of suppression that hinder your physical, emotional, and spiritual awareness. Natural diaphragmatic breathing, characterized by connected and continuous breaths, serves as the antidote to the constrictive breathing patterns that arise from suppression.

Suppression of your physical, emotional, or spiritual experiences often manifests in a held exhale and restricted inhalation. Such inhibited breathing restricts your intake of oxygen and contributes to the perpetuation of suppression. However, through connected breathing, you can reverse this process and restore harmony by embracing full and unrestricted breaths. This practice eliminates the energy required to hold and suppress your breath and the associated physical, emotional, and spiritual experiences. It interrupts the cycle of suppression, releasing the accumulated energy and facilitating a return to balance and equilibrium.

Practicing Breathing Love

Moving forward, 1 Corinthians chapter 13 mentions that if I have everything and not Love/ God, I have nothing. Breathing love energy is a practice that is both simple and innate. Therefore, it is important to realize that attracting this should be the first and foremost thing you need in order to build the ground for the rest of the exercises. Remember, conscious breathing is not just an exercise or a set of exercises; it is a lifestyle that, when you adopt and live it, will promote well-being and harmony in your life.

Let's get started:

Begin by setting aside 10-15 minutes each day for your Breathing Love (Spirit of God) session and extend the practice time to twice daily and the time per session to 20-30 minutes. Find a quiet and comfortable space where you can relax and focus.

Step 1: To create a conducive environment for your Breath of Love (Spirit of God) session, it is beneficial to incorporate relaxing and soothing music. Utilizing headphones can further enhance the experience by blocking out any unwanted sounds, allowing for a deeper sense of silence and stillness.

Step 2: Adopt a posture of relaxation by gently closing your eyes, releasing tension from your jaw, and softly opening your mouth. This physical alignment encourages a state of calmness and facilitates smooth and unhindered breathing.

Step 3: Commence the session by engaging in connected breaths for approximately 5 minutes. Allow your breath to flow in and out naturally while directing your attention to the rhythmic pattern of your breathing.

Step 4: Begin silently repeating the phrase "I Am/At Peace" on both the inhale and exhale of each breath. Allow the words to resonate within you.

Step 5: As you repeat the phrase, be open to any words, scenes, or feelings that come to your consciousness. Accept them without judgment or analysis.

Step 6: If your attention wanders, gently bring it back to the repeated phrase. Use it as your anchor and centering point.

Step 7: Continue this practice for 15-20 minutes, maintaining a steady rhythm of breathing and repetition of the phrase. Let each breath be a vehicle for experiencing stillness and inner peace.

Step 8: Embrace the stillness and inner peace that accompanies each Breath of Love (Spirit of God). Allow yourself to be present at the moment and cultivate a sense of serenity and tranquility.

Step 9: Conclude the session with one deep, slow breath and a slow exhale. Take a moment to acknowledge the transformative power of Love in your life.

Always keep in mind that the profound presence of Love has the power to transmute painful and fearful experiences into tranquil, affectionate, and wholesome memories. Embrace the practice of Breathing Love as a means to establish a connection with divine Love and truth, fostering your overall well-being and inner harmony.

Breathe Love Exercise for Safety and Peace

Step 1: Begin by closing your eyes and focusing on your breath. Engage in connected breaths for a duration of 5 minutes. Allow your breath to flow naturally, without any pauses between the inhalation and exhalation.

Step 2: Silently repeat non-directed phrases for 2 minutes with each breath, breathing in the Breath of Love (Spirit of God). For example, you can recite the phrase, "Build a rainbow bridge of Love and Truth to a safe and peaceful place."

Step 3: Surrender yourself to the scene and the feeling of safety and peace that arises in your mind. Accept this scene as a gift from the universal Love, embracing it as a significant aspect of your practice.

Step 4: Breath in the experience of safety and peace deeply. Allow the breath to carry the essence of these feelings throughout your body, filling you with a profound sense of calm and tranquility.

Step 5: Embrace the fullness of the scene by accepting all the colors, sounds, smells, and sensations associated with this safe and peaceful place. Immerse yourself in the sensory experience as you continue to breathe the Breath of Love (Spirit of God).

Step 6: Recognize that this scene can manifest in various settings, such as the mountains, a field, a forest, a beach, a room, or any other special place that resonates with your sense of safety and peace.

Step 7: Request that Love Energy be present in this safe and peaceful scene. Allow yourself to open up to the presence of universal love energy, welcoming it in whatever form it arrives with each Breath of Love (Spirit of God).

Step 8: Accept the presence of Perfect Love and Divine Truth that accompanies every breath you take. Embrace this profound energy as it permeates your being, connecting you to the core essence of Love and truth.

Step 9: Be receptive to any words, scenes, or feelings that emerge as you continuously breathe in Perfect Love and Divine Truth. Each breath becomes a vessel for deeper insights and connection to the divine.

Step 10: Ask for the ongoing acceptance and integration of Perfect Love and Divine Truth into your life. Invite these qualities to permeate every aspect of your being, nurturing your spiritual growth and well-being.

Step 11: Take in a deep, slow breath and slowly exhale. Slowly open your eyes.

Breathe Love Energy to Release Fear.

After being guided to the safe and peaceful place with the presence of God/Love, start with the following steps:

Step 1: Begin by inviting Love Energy to construct a "rainbow bridge" of Love and Truth that connects to your fears, regardless of their form or nature.

Step 2: Maintain the practice of breathing love and allow each wave of fear to emerge without resistance or judgment. Embrace the fears as they manifest in the form of words, scenes, or feelings.

Step 3: With each Breath/Spirit of Love/God, surrender and release your fears on every exhale. Let the love energy within you transform and dissolve the grip of fear.

Step 4: Continue this process with each breath, allowing each fear to arise and be released to the love energy. Embrace the healing power of Love as it permeates through every aspect of your being.

Step 5: As you breathe, consciously invite universal Truth to fill every cell in your body. Visualize and feel the presence of truth within you as you inhale the Breath of Love (Spirit of God).

Step 6: Deepen your connection to the truth by breathing the Light of Truth deeply into your bones. Imagine this light infusing your entire being, illuminating your inner wisdom and dispelling illusions.

Step 7: Use each breath as an opportunity to feast on the "food of the angels," breathing in Love. Embrace the nourishing and transformative qualities of Love that permeate your being.

Step 8: With each breath, allow perfect Love to fill your heart and soul. Open yourself to the unconditional Love that resides within and around you.

Step 9: Let this perfect Love flow into every cell of your body with each breath. Feel the love energy revitalizing and harmonizing your entire being.

Step 10: Accept and receive Love with each breath you take, and make a conscious choice to release fear with every breath. Remember that you have the power to let go of fear and embrace Love in each moment.

Step 11: Conclude the practice by taking a slow, deep breath and exhaling slowly. Open your eyes, feeling grounded and refreshed, carrying the energy of Love and truth with you into the world.

Harnessing the Power of Love to Align with Universal Truth

Begin breathing as before with eyes closed and a relaxed body posture:

Step 1: Ask Love to give you an image of a safe and peaceful place. Breathe Love into that safe and peaceful place.

Step 2: With each breath, ask that Universal Truth comes to every lie, distortion, distraction, illusion, confusion, denial, hurt, and pain.

Step 3: Breathe Love Energy and allow the word(s), scene(s), and feeling(s) to arise naturally.

Step 4: With each Breath/Spirit of Love/God, welcome and embrace each wave of Truth that comes to expose the lies, distortions, distractions, illusions, confusions, denials, hurts, and pains.

Step 5: Let the Perfect Love/God and Compassion fill your heart, soul, and every cell in your body.

Step 6: Breathe the power of perfect Love deep into your bones, infusing every part of your being with its transformative energy.

Step 7: With each exhale, surrender and release each lie, distortion, distraction, illusion, confusion, denial, hurt, and pain to the embrace of Perfect Love.

Step 8: With each breath, consciously choose to remember that Universal Truth accompanies every breath you take, offering liberation and freedom.

Step 9: Embrace this truth as you continue breathing, knowing that with each breath, you move closer to a state of profound freedom and inner alignment.

Step 10: Take a slow, deep breath, and exhale slowly. Open your eyes, feeling grounded and renewed, carrying the essence of Love and Truth with you as you navigate the world around you.

Ideal Times to Practice Breathing Love

Incorporating the practice of breathing love into specific times throughout your day can amplify the benefits and deepen your connection with love energy. Here are some optimal times to engage in breath love, along with their unique advantages:

1. **During Exercise:** Infuse your regular exercise routine with Breathing Love. The combination of physical movement and conscious breathing helps reverse energy and spirit suppression by increasing oxygen flow to every cell in your body and brain. This synergy enhances your overall well-being and elevates your exercise experience.

2. **Early Morning:** Rise early and dedicate 15-20 minutes to a Breathing Love session before engaging in your daily routine. This mindful practice sets a positive tone for the day, allowing you to cultivate inner peace and alignment with love energy from the very beginning. It establishes a strong foundation of Love, empowering you to navigate the challenges and opportunities that lie ahead.

3. **Before Bedtime:** Wind down your day by practicing breath love for 15-20 minutes just before bed. This is an opportune time to surrender, release, and let go of any lingering stress, tension, or negativity. Breathe in forgiveness for yourself and others, and invite the truth of Love to dissolve any barriers to your full prosperity and creativity. This practice promotes deep relaxation, peaceful sleep, and a refreshed state of mind for the following day.

4. **Throughout the Day:** Embrace a continuous practice of breathing love during your daily activities. Keep your eyes open and engage in connected breathing while silently repeating the phrase "I Am At Peace." This practice shifts your perception and response to life events, fostering a greater sense of calm and presence. Whether at work, during commutes, while shopping, in meetings, during conflicts, parenting, or even when making Love, breathing Love continuously transforms your experiences and nurtures a deeper connection with love energy.

By incorporating Breathing Love (Spirit of God) into these specific times, you can maximize the benefits of the practice and cultivate a more love-centered and fulfilling life experience. Embrace the power of conscious breathing to infuse love energy into every aspect of your day.

By dedicating yourselves to this practice, you unlock the ability to reverse suppression and bring balance to your physical, emotional, and spiritual awareness. Through natural diaphragmatic breathing, you release the energy that is bound by suppression and create space for Love to flow freely within you. You have witnessed how connected breathing and the repetition of non-directed phrases enable you to embrace the present moment, surrender your fears, and invite the transformative power of universal truth.

Breathing love is not limited to specific moments or formal sessions alone; it is a practice that can be woven seamlessly into your daily lives. Whether during exercise, in the stillness of the morning, or as you prepare to rest at night, the power of breath love is available to you at any given moment. By continuously infusing love energy into your experiences throughout the day, you deepen your connection to Love and expand your capacity for compassion, forgiveness, and peace.

As you embark on this journey of breathing love, remind yourself that it is not merely an isolated exercise but a way of being—a conscious choice to align yourselves with the essence of Love and truth. Through the power of your breath, you have the ability to transform yourselves and your worlds, one inhalation, and exhalation at a time. May the practice of breathing love lead you to a profound understanding of your own divinity and the boundless Love that surrounds you. Embrace this practice with an open heart and a willingness to surrender, and may it guide you toward a life filled with Love, joy, and inner harmony.

Chapter 5: Benefits of Conscious Breathing

The breath is an anchor amid the tides of endlessly changing circumstances and emotions. Your breath is your constant companion, something that will be with you for every moment that you live. When you make your home in breath, you take refuge in the eternal Spirit that lives within you. No one can take this place of belonging from you.

It is yours. This is home. This is where you live.

- Muller, 1992

Welcome to "The Benefits of Conscious Breathing," a section devoted to guiding you on the breath's capacity for transformation. Your breath remains steady in the broad terrain of life's constantly shifting circumstances and emotions, an unmoving anchor that travels with you through every second of existence. Your breath has an enormous power that you may use to feel comfortable and establish a connection with the everlasting Spirit that is within you. You will learn about the enormous benefits that conscious breathing may have on your physical, mental, and emotional health as you explore it more. Brace yourself for a journey that will awaken your senses, nourish your soul, and unveil the incredible sanctuary that resides within your own breath/Spirit.

For those of you who do not know, respiration is not just a mechanical process; it serves as a vital gateway to cellular vitality, enabling your body's essential functions to flourish. Through a series of intricate chemical reactions, oxygen plays a pivotal role in extracting energy from the food you consume, allowing your cells to thrive. This remarkable exchange within your body results in the production of adenosine triphosphate (ATP), the fundamental currency of cellular energy. Although glycolysis is a cellular process in which glucose (sugar) is partially broken-down using enzyme reactions to produce a small amount of ATP without requiring oxygen, it is the remarkable Krebs cycle that truly ignites the production of substantial energy. This cycle, powered by oxygen-rich respiration, plays a pivotal role in extracting a significant amount of ATP from food substances, allowing cells to thrive and function optimally. While glycolysis provides a modest energy yield, it is the synergistic combination of oxygen and the Krebs cycle that unleashes the full potential of cellular energy production. As a result of these cellular processes, carbon dioxide, and water are produced and carried away by the blood, highlighting the significance of oxygen.

Breath, particularly the oxygen it carries, plays a vital role in the conversion of food into the energy needed for life. Surprisingly, in the past Western culture had overlooked the significance of this energy process associated with breathing. In contrast, Eastern cultures have long embraced the concept of "inner breathing," a profound form of breathing that allows life energy to permeate every cell by deeply and completely filling the entire body (Lampman, 1999). This aspect of breathing may hold the key to your overall well-being, unlocking a potential source of vitality and balance within us. By recognizing and harnessing the power of breath, you can tap into this essential element and nurture your holistic health.

Every single day, you participate in the incredible process of breathing. It is fascinating to observe that, on average, a person takes approximately 12 to 20 breaths per minute, resulting in a remarkable total of 17,280 to 28,800 breaths within the span of a single 24-hour day. However, the actual number of breaths can vary depending on factors such as physical activity, stress levels, and overall health. As for the volume of air inhaled, it is estimated that an average adult breathes in about 6 to 10 liters of air per minute. This amounts to around 8,640 to 14,400 liters (or approximately 2282 to 3,804 gallons) of air in a day. This continuous rhythm of inhalation and exhalation sustains your life, providing a constant flow of oxygen to nourish your body and fuel its vital functions. The sheer magnitude of these breaths highlights the profound significance of this innate and essential act.

The process of breathing is not only limited to inhalation and exhalation, but it also plays an integral part in your body's natural detoxification mechanism, contributing to the elimination of toxins alongside other bodily functions such as perspiration, defecation, and urination. Oxygen is a vital component of breathing and, indeed, plays a crucial role in nourishing your system, enabling the optimal functioning of your body, it supports the metabolic processes that convert nutrients from food into energy.

Recognizing the criticality of oxygen, it comes as no surprise that it takes precedence when it enters your bloodstream. Its immediate distribution throughout your body highlights its indispensability. While the human body can endure several days without food, mere hours without heat, and a few days without liquids, the absence of oxygen presents a dire situation. Within a mere four minutes, the lack of oxygen can inflict severe brain damage and, ultimately, lead to death. Every second that passes without oxygen, cells begin to perish, stressing the pressing need for a constant supply of this life-sustaining element to every cell in your body. By embracing the art of proper breathing, you empower cellular activity, rejuvenate your strength, and kindle the essence of your existence (Lampman, 1999).

The breath possesses a remarkable dichotomy, serving as both a voluntary and involuntary bodily function. Its voluntary nature allows it to act as a bridge connecting your conscious and unconscious mental processes. By mindfully regulating your breath, you gain access to a profound realm of self-awareness, aligning your body and mind in harmony. The diaphragm and intercostal chest muscles play vital roles in the symphony of your Breath/Spirit, facilitating its movement and fostering a sense of interconnectedness with the rhythm of your heart. It would not be wrong to say that your breaths, when harmonized with the heart, give rise to emotional breaths.

Emotional Breath:

The intimate relationship between your breath and your emotions is referred to as emotional breath. It acknowledges that your emotional state may affect your breath, which in turn can affect your emotions. When you are nervous or calm, you may breathe shallowly and quickly, while on the other hand, you may breathe deeply and slowly. Conscious breathing exercises may also be utilized to control and affect your emotions. You can consciously change the way you breathe to have a soothing influence on your emotions, increasing relaxation and lowering tension and anxiety. The concept of "emotional breath" recognizes the complex connection between your breathing and your emotional health, emphasizing the possibility of using your Breath/Spirit as a tool for emotional control, self-awareness, and personal growth.

It is noteworthy to observe that at the heart or soul level, your emotions deeply influence your sexual feelings, personal connections, and interactions with others. It is in alignment with natural laws that many spiritual teachers emphasize the utmost importance of diaphragmatic breathing, guiding you to use your breath as a powerful tool to "open your heart." By consciously engaging in this form of breathing, you can unlock the profound influence your breath has on your emotional well-being, fostering a deeper connection with yourself and others.

Spiritual Breath:

Similarly, spiritual breath refers to using conscious breathing techniques to connect with your spiritual essence, accessing inner wisdom, and deepening your sense of interconnectedness. By engaging in intentional and mindful breathing practices, you can cultivate a profound awareness, inner peace, and a greater understanding of your spiritual nature. It is a pathway to explore the transcendent aspects of your existence, fostering personal growth and facilitating a transformative journey of self-discovery.

By recognizing the profound interplay between your breath and emotions and embracing the spiritual potential of your breath, you can embark on a transformative journey. Through conscious breathing, you empower yourself to tap into the depths of your emotional world, nurturing personal growth and cultivating meaningful connections with your inner self. The harmony between conscious breathing, emotional breath, and spiritual breath forms a powerful synergy, offering you enhanced well-being.

Embracing this transformative journey into the realm of conscious breathing, where the Breath/Spirit becomes a gateway to vitality, self-awareness, and inner harmony, is essential not only for your physical health but also for your emotional and spiritual well-being. With each inhalation and exhalation, you embark on a profound exploration of your body's boundless potential. Prepare to cultivate a deeper understanding of the remarkable benefits that conscious breathing can bestow upon your life by impacting your life.

Physical Benefits of Conscious Breathing

1. **Improved lung function:** Conscious breathing involves deep, controlled breathing techniques that focus on expanding the lungs to their full capacity. By purposefully taking deep breaths that involve the diaphragm, you can elevate your lung function, amplify oxygen intake, and optimize the distribution of oxygen throughout the body. This can result in enhanced respiratory well-being,

heightened energy levels, and an improved overall supply of oxygen to organs and tissues. A study published by Hamasaki (2020) in the Journal of Medicines (Basel), titled "Effects of Diaphragmatic Breathing on Health: A Narrative Review," investigated the impact of a diaphragmatic breathing program on lung function in individuals with asthma. The study found that participants who engaged in diaphragmatic breathing techniques experienced notable enhancements in lung function, including increased peak expiratory flow rate and improved forced vital capacity. This research highlights the positive effect of controlled breathing on respiratory health, as detailed in the study by Hamasaki (2020).[1]

2. **Boosts the immune system:** Chronic stress can weaken the immune system, making the body more susceptible to illnesses and infections. Conscious breathing practices help activate the relaxation response and reduce stress levels, which in turn positively impacts the immune system. By reducing stress hormones and promoting a sense of calm, conscious breathing supports immune function and strengthens the body's natural defense mechanisms.

3. **Reduced cardiovascular strain**: Conscious breathing techniques, such as slow and controlled breathing, have been shown to have a positive impact on cardiovascular health. By practicing deep and intentional breathing, you can lower blood pressure, reduce the heart rate, and decrease the workload on the heart. This, in turn, can lower the risk of cardiovascular diseases such as hypertension and

---

[1] Hamasaki H. (2020). Effects of Diaphragmatic Breathing on Health: A Narrative Review. Medicines (Basel, Switzerland), 7(10), 65. https://doi.org/10.3390/medicines7100065

heart disease.[2] Consistent practice of conscious breathing can help promote a healthier cardiovascular system and improve overall heart health.[3]

4. **Improved digestion:** Conscious breathing can activate the parasympathetic nervous system, often referred to as the "rest and digest" response. When activated, this system promotes relaxation, aids digestion, and supports optimal gastrointestinal function. By incorporating conscious breathing techniques into your routine, you can stimulate the parasympathetic nervous system, which can lead to improved digestion, reduced symptoms of gastrointestinal disorders, and a greater sense of overall digestive well-being. It can help alleviate issues such as bloating, gas, and constipation.[4]

By incorporating conscious breathing practices into your daily life, you can experience these remarkable physical benefits. Consistent practice is key to unlocking the full potential of conscious breathing and integrating it into your overall well-being. Embrace the power of your breath and explore the transformative impact it can have on your physical health.

---

[2] Yau, K. K., & Loke, A. Y. (2021). Effects of diaphragmatic deep breathing exercises on prehypertensive or hypertensive adults: A literature review. Complementary therapies in clinical practice, 43, 101315. https://doi.org/10.1016/j.ctcp.2021.101315

[3] Naik, G. S., Gaur, G. S., & Pal, G. K. (2018). Effect of Modified Slow Breathing Exercise on Perceived Stress and Basal Cardiovascular Parameters. International Journal of Yoga, 11(1), 53–58. https://doi.org/10.4103/ijoy.IJOY_41_16

[4] University of Michigan Health. (n.d.). Diaphragmatic Breathing for GI Patients. Retrieved from https://www.uofmhealth.org/conditions-treatments/digestive-and-liver-health/diaphragmatic-breathing-gi-patients

Moreover, conscious breathing not only has a profound impact on your physical well-being but also holds significant benefits for your mental health and overall sense of wellness. Let us explore in detail the mental benefits of conscious breathing supported by research:

1. **Reduced anxiety and stress:** Research has shown that conscious breathing techniques can activate the body's relaxation response, leading to a reduction in anxiety and stress levels. When you engage in deep, slow breathing, you stimulate the parasympathetic nervous system, which counters the effects of the sympathetic nervous system responsible for the body's stress response. This activation of the relaxation response promotes a sense of calmness, lowers cortisol levels, and helps alleviate feelings of anxiety and stress. In a study by Richard et al. published in the Journal of Alternative and complementary medicine, the authors studied the effects of Sudarshan Kriya Yogic breathing, a form of conscious breathing. The findings indicate that SKY can have positive effects on various psychological and stress-related disorders. The technique is effective for the treatment of conditions such as stress, anxiety, post-traumatic stress disorder (PTSD), depression, stress-related medical illnesses, substance abuse, and rehabilitation of criminal offenders. The technique is also found to have a positive impact on mood, attention, mental focus, and stress tolerance.[5]

---

[5] Brown, R. P., & Gerbarg, P. L. (2005). Sudarshan Kriya Yogic breathing in the treatment of stress, anxiety, and depression. Part II--

2. **Increased focus and mental clarity:** Conscious breathing practices have been found to enhance focus, concentration, and mental clarity. Conscious breathing supports optimal brain function by improving oxygenation and blood flow to the brain. Research suggests that deep, intentional breathing techniques improve functions like decision-making, problem-solving, and attention.[6] This boost in oxygen and improved blood flow helps sharpen cognitive abilities, increase mental alertness, and enhance overall focus.

3. **Improved sleep quality:** Conscious breathing techniques, such as deep breathing, meditation, and progressive muscle relaxation, have been linked to improved sleep quality. Research indicates that incorporating these practices into a bedtime routine can help calm the mind, reduce insomnia, and promote restful sleep. By inducing a state of relaxation, conscious breathing prepares the body for rest, eases racing thoughts, and encourages a deeper and more rejuvenating sleep. This, in turn, leads to improved overall sleep health and a greater sense of well-being during waking hours. The study titled "Effectiveness of Progressive Muscle Relaxation and Deep Breathing Exercise on Pain, Disability, and

---

clinical applications and Guidelines. Journal of Alternative and complementary medicine (New York, N.Y.), 11(4), 711–717. https://doi.org/10.1089/acm.2005.11.711

[6] Ma, X., Yue, Z. Q., Gong, Z. Q., Zhang, H., Duan, N. Y., Shi, Y. T., Wei, G. X., & Li, Y. F. (2017). The Effect of Diaphragmatic Breathing on Attention, Negative Affect, and Stress in Healthy Adults. Frontiers in Psychology, pp. 8, 874. https://doi.org/10.3389/fpsyg.2017.00874

Sleep Among Patients With Chronic Tension-Type Headache" conducted a randomized control trial to evaluate the impact of progressive muscle relaxation and deep breathing exercises on individuals with chronic tension-type headache. Among the 169 participants, 84 individuals underwent the intervention and experienced significant improvements in pain severity, disability, and sleep quality after a period of 12 weeks. The findings of this study suggest that the implementation of progressive muscle relaxation and deep breathing exercises can be effective in alleviating pain, reducing disability, and enhancing sleep among patients with chronic tension-type headaches (Gopichandran et al., 2021).[7]

4. **Enhanced mood and emotional regulation:** Conscious breathing exercises can have a positive impact on mood and emotional well-being. By regulating the breath, you influence the autonomic nervous system, which plays a crucial role in emotional regulation. Studies have shown that conscious breathing techniques, such as diaphragmatic breathing and alternate nostril breathing, can help reduce symptoms of depression, anxiety, and emotional distress. These practices

---

[7] Gopichandran, L., Srivastsava, A. K., Vanamail, P., Kanniammal, C., Valli, G., Mahendra, J., & Dhandapani, M. (2021). Effectiveness of Progressive Muscle Relaxation and Deep Breathing Exercise on Pain, Disability, and Sleep Among Patients With Chronic Tension-Type Headache: A Randomized Control Trial. Holistic Nursing Practice. Advanced online publication. https://doi.org/10.1097/HNP.0000000000000460

promote a sense of inner calm, balance emotional states, and support overall emotional well-being.

Conscious breathing is a powerful tool for managing mental health and promoting overall wellness. By incorporating conscious breathing practices into your daily lives, you can reduce anxiety and stress, improve focus and mental clarity, enhance sleep quality, and regulate your emotions more effectively. Embracing the transformative potential of conscious breathing allows you to nurture your mental well-being and cultivate a greater sense of inner peace and balance.

Controlled Breathing Techniques

1. **Diaphragmatic Breathing:** This technique involves consciously engaging the diaphragm, the primary muscle responsible for breathing, by expanding the belly on inhalation and contracting it on exhalation. It promotes deep and efficient breathing.

2. **Box Breathing:** Also known as square breathing, this technique involves inhaling, holding the breath, exhaling, and holding again, all for equal counts of time.

3. **Alternate Nostril Breathing:** This technique involves using the fingers to alternately close one nostril while breathing in through the other, and vice versa. It balances the flow of energy in the body and promotes a sense of balance and harmony.

4. **4-7-8 Breathing:** This technique involves inhaling deeply through the nose for a count of 4, holding the breath for a count of 7, and exhaling slowly through the mouth for a count of 8. It promotes relaxation and stress reduction.

5. **Breath Counting:** This technique involves focusing on the breath and counting each inhalation and exhalation. It helps enhance concentration and mindfulness.

Chapter 6: Fear - A Hindrance in the Ultimate Love Experience

Be anxious for nothing.... And the Peace of God, which passeth all understanding shall keep your hearts and minds through Jesus Christ

Philippians 4:6-7

Fear is an innate and powerful emotion that all humans experience at some or the other point in their lives. It acts as a survival mechanism that is built into your body to protect you from threats and hazards. It is intriguing to know that discovering how fear operates may empower you to control and conquer it, allowing you to live a more purposeful and peaceful life.

You must know that it is the perception that causes fear when your brain detects a threat or danger, whether it is genuine or imagined. The amygdala, a little almond-shaped region in your brain, plays a crucial role in the processing of fear. It functions as an alarm system, rapidly evaluating incoming data and generating signals to trigger the fight-or-flight response. When the fight-or-flight response is triggered, a complex series of physiological changes occur within your body. The primary players in this response are the sympathetic nervous system and the adrenal glands.

The sympathetic nervous system kicks into action, releasing stress hormones such as adrenaline and noradrenaline. These hormones quickly prepare your body for action. Here's what happens:

1. **Increased heart rate:** Your heart beats faster to pump oxygen-rich blood to your muscles and vital organs, providing them with the energy they need to respond effectively.

2. **Rapid breathing:** Your breathing rate increases to take in more oxygen, which helps fuel your muscles and increases alertness.

3. **Muscle tension:** Your muscles become tense and ready for action. This tension allows for quick movements and increased strength.

4. **Dilation of pupils:** Your pupils widen to allow more light into your eyes, enhancing your vision and peripheral awareness.

5. **Sweating:** Your body starts to sweat, which helps regulate body temperature during physical exertion and may also make it more difficult for a potential predator to grip you.

6. **Suppressed digestion:** The fight-or-flight response diverts resources away from non-essential bodily functions, including digestion, so that energy can be directed toward the immediate threat.

7. **Heightened senses:** Your senses become more acute, enabling you to perceive potential threats more quickly and accurately.

These physiological adjustments are made to give you the vigor and stamina you need to react appropriately.

There are two sorts of fear:

1. **Natural:** Phobias that are present from birth are innate and include phobias of loud noises and falling
2. **Taught:** On the other hand, acquired anxieties are brought on by past traumas or cultural factors. For instance, you could grow to dread dogs if you had a bad encounter with them when you were a youngster. Similarly, fear of abandonment, fear of failing, and fear of losing loved ones are all acquired fears which can be treated.

Initially, it can be challenging to discern and categorize your fears, distinguishing between those that are inherent or learned and determining which fears hold genuine substance and which are merely transient bubbles. You are not to blame for this, as it is not something that arises overnight. Instead, it is a natural part of the human experience that develops over the years, gradually becoming deeply ingrained within your brain.

The fear response has evolved over millions of years of human experience, during which survival was a constant concern. Early humans spent their lives either hunting for food or avoiding becoming prey themselves. Those individuals whose Central Nervous Systems were slow to respond were naturally selected out of the gene pool as they struggled to secure their own survival. As a result, we are all descendants of ancestors with highly sensitive Central Nervous Systems, particularly the Autonomic Nervous System. This sensitivity means that even the slightest hint of a real or imagined threat triggers the rapid release of powerful hormones like adrenaline and cortisol, activating the "fight or flight" response within milliseconds (Borysenko, 1987).

Fear can also become maladaptive when it starts to have a significant impact on your daily life and start preventing you from pursuing your goals and dreams. It is important to recognize that fear is often based on anticipation and speculation rather than concrete evidence. It would not be wrong to say that most of your fears are like bubbles that appear substantial and overwhelming, but upon closer examination, they can be fragile and easily popped. By understanding this, you can begin to challenge and reframe your fearful and threatening thoughts.

Fortunately, the level of existential threats our ancestors faced, such as life-threatening encounters with animals or hostile tribes, has significantly diminished in today's world. However, it is regrettable that modern-day survival challenges often manifest in different forms. These challenges are primarily reflected in the intense pressure to navigate the complexities of the fast-paced society. They come in the guise of stressors like financial burdens, relationship difficulties, the fear of succeeding or failing, and the overwhelming weight of anxious anticipation. Since the "fight or flight" response is often not a viable option in these situations, you often find yourselves in a heightened state of physical arousal, experiencing what is commonly known as the "freeze" or "fawn" response. Many of you remain unaware of the underlying fear associated with the stressors you face in modern life, even though current research strongly suggests that unmanaged stress (fear) can lead to physical, mental, and spiritual ailments.

Fear is constrained by the boundaries of time, space, and matter, permeating your experiences across the past, present, and future. You tend to project your fearful memories from past encounters onto your current reality and even extend them into your anticipated future. The language of fear encompasses a wide range of expressions, including notions of impossibility, limitations, self-doubt, regret, and self-criticism. Phrases like "I can't," "if only," "always," "never," "ought to," "should," "doubt," "shame," "guilt," "blame," "separation," "judgment," criticism," and the persistent belief of "I'm not good enough" all contribute to the vocabulary of fear.

Numerous fears find their origins in unsettling past experiences, detrimental teachings, traumatic experiences, and challenging relationships, particularly those encountered during childhood. These fears tend to extend their influence into both the present moment and your anticipated future (Seamands, 1985). Emotional trauma has the capacity to amplify and magnify all fears, transcending individual circumstances. When you experience emotional trauma, it can have a profound impact on your perception and response to fear. Traumatic events can create deep-rooted wounds that intensify and generalize fears, making them more pervasive and impactful across various aspects of life. This amplification of fears on a global scale highlights the profound and interconnected nature of emotional trauma and its effects on your psychological well-being even when you have grown up and apparently let go of those harsh memories.

It is crucial to know that the free flow of life energy, encompassing your physical, emotional, and spiritual aspects, can be impeded by the presence of fear and resistance rooted in negative and self-perpetuating beliefs. These beliefs, often based on falsehoods, hinder the full expression of your true self. The rapid pace of change and constant transitions in modern life can further contribute to the fear of the unknown, eroding your faith in the process (Virtue, 1997). Fear is a deceptive illusion that suggests a disconnection from Love/God. It often feels involuntary and beyond your control, weaving its way into your thoughts and emotions. Fear is essentially a mental state characterized by a mindset of imitation, scarcity, and unhappiness (Holmes, 1938). Unbeknownst to you, fear perpetuates itself by shaping your perceptions and influencing your experiences in a continuous cycle (Zukav, 1989).

The illusory nature of the ego or self, influenced by fear, is reinforced by a cascade of emotions that accompany it. Anger, rage, vengefulness, hatred, jealousy, loneliness, spite, sorrow, despair, grief, regret, greed, lust, arrogance, alienation, self-pity, lethargy, guilt, resentment, inferiority, and superiority all contribute to this emotional reinforcement. Such emotions lead to choices and behaviors that are projected onto yourselves and others, including lying, manipulation, violence, brutality, impatience, and judgment.

This fear-driven state, rooted in the "fight or flight" survival mentality and the perception of scarcity, places a strong emphasis on external power and a need for control. Much of your culture reflects this competitive pursuit of external power fueled by fear. However, this self-serving love and possessiveness ultimately drain your energy and perpetuate patterns of conditional love (Myss, 1997).

It is essential to recognize that you play an active role in creating your own fear through the belief in separation from Love Energy. By accepting responsibility for your fear and consciously choosing to correct it, you have the power to transform your life (Schulman and Thetford, 1975). Although you may continue to complain about fear, remain persistent in choosing it, and in doing so, you perpetuate a cycle of miscreation, where events align with your fear-based perceptions.

There are various reasons why humans tend to continue selecting fear and perpetuating a cycle of creating undesirable outcomes. These reasons are rooted in complex psychological and emotional dynamics that influence your thoughts, behaviors, and perceptions. Here are a few common factors:

1. **Familiarity:** Fear can become familiar and comfortable, even if it is unpleasant. It becomes a known state, and humans tend to gravitate towards what they know, even if it hinders their growth and well-being.

   As an illustration: Imagine a person who grew up in a highly critical and demanding environment. They became accustomed to constantly feeling afraid of making mistakes and facing harsh judgment. As they entered adulthood, this fear of criticism and failure became their comfort zone.

   Despite the unpleasantness of living in constant fear, they find it difficult to step outside of their comfort

63

zone and embrace new opportunities or take risks. The familiarity of fear outweighs the potential for growth and well-being. They gravitate towards what they know, even if it hinders their personal and professional development. Sometimes such people would not even know that they are living in fear and that their personal development is being hindered until they are counseled, encouraged, or enlightened by the truth.

2. **Conditioning and past experiences:** Negative experiences and conditioning from the past can shape your beliefs and expectations. If you have encountered painful or traumatic events, your mind may associate similar circumstances with fear, leading you to choose fear as a way to protect yourself from potential harm.

3. **Belief systems:** Your belief systems play a significant role in shaping your choices. If you hold deep-seated beliefs that reinforce fear-based thinking, such as beliefs in scarcity, unworthiness, or a hostile world, you are more likely to continue choosing fear and perpetuating its cycle.

   For example, A person who had a past romantic relationship that ended in heartbreak and betrayal. This experience left them with a deep-seated belief that they are unworthy of love and that relationships are inherently painful and unreliable. As they move forward in their life, this fear-based belief system continues to shape their choices and behaviors. They may find themselves avoiding potential romantic partners or sabotaging new relationships out of fear of being hurt again. Their belief in unworthiness and fear of vulnerability keeps them stuck in a cycle of choosing fear.

Despite opportunities for love and connection, they unconsciously gravitate towards situations that align with their fear-based beliefs. This perpetuates a pattern where their choices, actions, and perceptions reinforce their initial belief system, creating a self-fulfilling prophecy.

4. **Social and cultural influences:** Society and culture often reinforce fear-based narratives and behaviors. From media messages to societal norms, you may be surrounded by fear-inducing influences that can validate and perpetuate your own fears.

    For instance: There may be cultural pressure to conform to certain standards of success, beauty, or social status. This fear of not measuring up to societal ideals can lead to anxiety, self-doubt, and a constant striving for approval. Moreover, advertising and marketing techniques frequently capitalize on fear by highlighting potential risks or problems that their products or services claim to solve. Whether it's fear of aging, financial instability, or social rejection, these fear-inducing messages can manipulate consumer behavior and perpetuate a culture of fear-driven consumption.

5. **Self-protection**: Paradoxically, fear can offer a sense of protection. It creates a barrier that you believe shields you from potential harm or disappointment. Even if fear limits your experiences and potential, it can provide a false sense of security.

As an exemplification: Imagine a person who has a fear of public speaking. They feel anxious and overwhelmed at the thought of speaking in front of a large audience. As a result, they consistently avoid opportunities to give presentations or share their ideas in a public setting.

While their fear of public speaking limits their personal growth and professional opportunities, it also provides them with a perceived sense of protection. By avoiding public speaking engagements, they believe they are shielding themselves from potential embarrassment, judgment, or failure. In their mind, fear acts as a protective barrier, keeping them safe from the perceived risks and negative outcomes associated with public speaking.

6. **Lack of awareness:** Many individuals may not fully realize the extent to which they are choosing fear or the impact it has on their lives. Unconscious patterns and conditioning can keep them trapped in fear-based responses without conscious awareness.

   To give an example: Someone who grew up in a household where they witnessed their parents constantly worrying about money and expressing fear of financial instability. As a result, they internalized these fear-based patterns and developed an unconscious belief that money is scarce and difficult to come by.

   Throughout their adult life, these people find themselves experiencing financial struggles and setbacks. They may have difficulty finding stable employment, struggle to save money, and feel constant anxiety about their financial future. However, they are unaware of the underlying belief in scarcity that is driving these patterns.

These unconscious fears have a profound impact on your intimate relationships, making it challenging to establish a deep and meaningful connection. The magnitude and significance of these fears within relationships have been measured by Sheehan (1994) using an instrument developed by Jampolsky and Feldman (1979). These fears, which operate at a subconscious level, can manifest in various ways and hinder the establishment of intimacy. They can create a fear of vulnerability, leading individuals to build emotional walls and prevent genuine emotional connection. Fear of rejection may cause individuals to withhold their true selves and limit their authenticity within the relationship. Fear of abandonment can lead to clinginess or an excessive need for reassurance, ultimately pushing partners away. Fear of intimacy itself can result in emotional distance or a fear of getting too close. These unconscious fears impact your relationships by creating difficulties in trust-building, open communication, and emotional availability, ultimately posing challenges in establishing an intimate connection.

FEARS	MANIFESTATION / EXTENT
Merger	1. Fear of Intimate Relationships: 2. Loss of identity and self-expression 3. Avoidance of communication, commitment, and negotiation 4. Perfectionistic tendencies and a need for control
Abandonment	1. Fear of Rejection. 2. Maintaining distance and avoiding deep commitment. 3. Engaging in shallow relationships 4. Feeling jealous and insecure
Exposure	1. Fear of exposure of low self-esteem and shame. 2. Believing oneself to be weak, stupid, undesirable, inadequate, bad, or ugly. 3. Blaming others instead of facing personal truths.
Attack	1. Fear of Emotional and Physical Hurt

	2. Associating love with pain and hurt due to past experiences 3. Developing a fear of emotional vulnerability
Own Self Destructive Impulse	1. Fear of Own Destructive Impulses 2. Fear of one's own anger, rage, and potential to hurt others. 3. Engaging in self-defeating behaviors 4. Nit-picking, nagging, and whining

In his work, Sheehan highlights how fear, stemming from ignorance, pride, and self-doubt, becomes a significant barrier to establishing intimate relationships. When these fears go unidentified and unaddressed, their impact on your relationships can be deeply destructive, causing you to even develop a fear of Love (God) itself. It is crucial, therefore, to recognize and confront these fears in order to foster healthy and meaningful connections with others, as well as to restore your ability to experience the profound love and connection that intimate relationships can bring.

It is through the conscious choice to move away from fear and align with Love/God that you can break free from these patterns and embrace a more authentic and fulfilling existence. By letting go of fear and choosing Love/God, you open yourselves to a world of possibilities rooted in compassion, connection, and harmonious coexistence. In the next chapter, you will get to delve deeper into the concept of Perfect Love and its transformative power. You will explore how Perfect Love, which is inherently devoid of fear, can be harnessed as a guiding force to cast out fear from your lives. By understanding and practicing Perfect Love, you will discover practical techniques and strategies to cultivate a state of love-centered consciousness, enabling you to overcome fear and embrace a more authentic and fulfilling existence.

Some Facts about Understanding Fears in Relationships

Fears as a Universal Aspect of Relationships:

- Fears are inherent in all relationships to some degree.
- Each person brings their own set of fears into a relationship.

The Complexity of Fears in Relationships:

- Relationships can involve multiple fears simultaneously.
- Different fears may hold varying levels of significance in different relationships.

Dynamics and Evolution of Relationship Fears:

- Fears within relationships can change over time and in response to life events.
- Certain experiences or milestones may trigger the intensification of fears.

The Influence of Stress on Relationship Fears:

- Increased stress levels can heighten fears within relationships.

Stressful situations may amplify the impact of existing

Chapter 7: Overcoming Fear Through Perfect Love

There is no fear in Love, but perfect Love casts out fear. For fear has to do with punishment, and whoever fears has not been perfected in Love.

−1 John 4:18

In your journey through life, fear often lurks in the shadows, obstructing your path and holding you back from reaching your full potential. As discussed in the previous chapter, fear can manifest itself in various forms, paralyzing you with doubt, anxiety, and uncertainty. It can prevent you from pursuing your dreams, embracing new opportunities, or forging meaningful connections with others. But within the depths of your hearts lies a powerful antidote to fear: perfect Love.

Love, in its purest form, has the ability to dissolve the walls you build around yourself, allowing you to step into the unknown with courage and resilience. It is a force that illuminates your darkest corners, casting out the shadows of fear and replacing them with hope, compassion, and understanding. As you embark on your journey toward inner peace, personal growth, and spiritual empowerment, you'll encounter a powerful belief that Love energy is the ultimate force behind all that exists. Drawing inspiration from Peck's work in 1978, you will come to understand that Love is your will to extend yourself for the purpose of nurturing your own or another's spiritual growth (p. 81). It's fueled by Perfect Love and sets in motion a beautiful cycle of love empowerment that starts and preserves within you.

Easier said than done, right? No one can deny the fact that all along, you must have learned various fears that may not be overcome easily, making it difficult to fully love. As you go through life, influenced by the idea of competition and survival of the fittest, you may start to believe that there is a lack of Love. You may think that when you give Love, you lose it, and you might feel like your inner well of Love is always running dry, especially with those who are unable to reciprocate the same Love you share with them and those who return Love with hate and hurt (Jampolsky 1979). Fear becomes a measure of the Love you give and receive, underscoring the importance of letting go of fear in order to truly embrace and experience Love in your life. Consequently, in an attempt to alleviate this perceived void, individuals may turn to different worldly diversions. These diversions may involve seeking approval and validation in relationships, indulging in physical pleasures, pursuing wealth and achievement, asserting dominance over others, keeping excessively occupied, or even encountering mental and physical health challenges. This entire picture may have been your experience up till now, but certainly, that's not how it really is, and it's definitely not the universal truth. Here is a universal truth: Say it out loud. *Fear cannot hinder my desire to love. Giving Love to others cannot put me at a loss or depletion.*

First of all, you will have to change your paradigm of fear and Love.

- Fear is not constant, but Love is.
- If you realize the power of Love, fear cannot hold you back.
- You are born with Love but not with most fear that you experience.

The teachings of unconditional Love remind you of something important: you are intrinsically intertwined with Perfect Love, created in the very image of Love itself. This realization, as echoed by Caroline Myss and countless spiritual teachings, reveals something remarkable within you, and that is the incredible potential to love yourself and others without feeling depleted. But how can this be?

Here is the answer to this. With each breath you take, you are refilled with the energy of Love, ensuring that you have an endless source to draw from. As you wholeheartedly accept this reality, you'll find that every event and circumstance in life becomes an invitation—an opportunity to experience and express Love in its most genuine and powerful form because instead of surviving, you will be living life to its fullest.

It is essential to understand that you cannot wait for Love to emerge fully only after you have eradicated fear entirely. It is the other way around; to eliminate fear from your lives, you require Love, and you have to nurture the existing Love whose awareness you have just received. You must have heard that perfect *Love casts out fear*. Hence, you need to learn the way of Perfect Love to release all the fears that you have been harboring in your life.

But what is Perfect Love? And what is the process of liberating fear through Love?

Well, the Bible says that "*God is love; and he that dwelleth in love dwelleth in God, and God in him*" 1 John 4:16. Perfect Love, a concept that transcends complete description, holds within it a myriad of extraordinary qualities that shape your understanding of this remarkable force. While capturing the entirety of Love's essence is a formidable task, you can uncover some universal truths that provide glimpses into its profound nature. These unfolding truths can serve as guiding principles in your quest for personal growth, inner peace, and spiritual fulfillment. If God is Love, then Love encompasses all the attributes associated with God. And you will learn that Love is eternal, omnipresent, all-powerful, all-knowing, the Creator, the Counselor, the Healer, the Redeemer, and the Source of all goodness. In the Bible, Love is portrayed as patient, kind, devoid of jealousy and boasting, not arrogant, characterized by compassion, selflessness, forgiveness, and a focus on the truth. Love bears all things, believes in all things, hopes in all things, endures all things, and never fails (1 Corinthians 13:4-8).

The process of liberating fear through Love is an ongoing journey. It begins by recognizing and acknowledging your fears, particularly those rooted in past experiences of conditional Love or hurtful encounters. By cultivating genuine Love for yourselves and others, you create an environment that fosters healing and growth. Love empowers you to let go of fear's grip by providing a safe space for vulnerability, compassion, and forgiveness. When you have begun your journey in Love, fear gradually loses its power as you begin to grow stronger. It is a continuous process of consciously choosing Love over fear, nurturing your capacity to love unconditionally, and allowing Love to permeate every aspect of your life.

In order to experience a true release from fear, it is essential to follow a transformative process:

1. **Know Your Fears:** Begin by acknowledging and understanding your fears. Take the time to identify and become aware of the specific fears that hold you back.
2. **Fear is Lack of Love:** Recognize that fear emerges from a sense of lacking Love. Understand that when Love is absent or diminished, fear tends to take its place.
3. **Embrace the Remedy, Perfect Love:** Perfect Love encompasses unconditional Love, compassion, and acceptance. It is through cultivating and embracing this divine Love that fear begins to lose its grip.
4. **Only Love Can Transform:** Remember that only Love has the power to bring about genuine transformation. As you actively choose Love over fear, you create space for healing, growth, and liberation.

By following this process, you open the door to releasing fear and inviting Love into your life. It is through the power of Perfect Love that fear loses its hold, enabling you to live a more courageous, joyful, and fulfilling existence.

Universal truths about Perfect Love

1. Giving Love allows you to receive Love in return.

2. When you offer Love to others, you simultaneously nurture yourself with Love.
3. Love embodies abundance, prosperity, and the power of creation.
4. You are originally created in a state of Perfect Love, with Love intertwined within your very breath.
5. With every breath you take, you infuse every cell in your body with the essence of Perfect Love.
6. The Love contained within each breath is infinite and can never be depleted.

In truth, Perfect Love is all about the connection between giving and receiving, the amazing ability to create abundance, and the Love that resides within you. It's like an endless well that gets refilled with each breath you take. To genuinely extend Love to others, an essential truth must be acknowledged that you cannot give what you do not possess. Indeed, you are intrinsically connected to Perfect Love, created in the very image of Love itself. The presence of Love within you is inherent and ever-present. However, the notion of self-love emphasizes the importance of nurturing and cultivating that existing Love within yourself. Therefore, the journey of Love that begins within yourself requires the cultivation and nurturing of Love in your own being. Through acts of self-love, acceptance, and a deep appreciation for your inherent worthiness, you unlock the wellspring of Love residing within. This self-nurturing journey becomes the foundation from which you can authentically and wholeheartedly share Love with others.

Self-love is an integral aspect of your ability to both give and receive Love. Embracing self-love often entails going through a phase of self-centeredness where many of you eventually reach a point where this self-indulgent, egocentric mindset, characterized by prioritizing your own needs and seeking instant gratification, disregards the consequences. You must learn that this type of Love no longer brings you satisfaction, companionship, or happiness (particularly when it comes to how you perceive yourself). This kind of self-serving Love and possessiveness depletes your energy instead of replenishing it. However, it's important to recognize that you possess the power to embrace and accept yourself just as you are. By doing so, you can let go of the false beliefs and illusions that are tied to conditional self-love. You don't have to stay trapped in negative aspects of fear, such as bitterness, jealousy, or the inability to forgive. You have the ability to free yourself from these limitations and experience love in its purest and most transformative form. You have the power to choose self-love unconditionally by listening to your heart. When you embrace unconditional self-love, you naturally extend that Love to others without conditions or limitations.

In your closest relationships, you may encounter anger, betrayal, criticism, or a lack of acceptance. These experiences can shape your understanding of Love and influence how you perceive the concept of "God." However, when you consciously breathe in Love, you can turn inward, seeking solace in silence and solitude. It is in this space that you will discover a transformative kind of Love that has the potential to revolutionize your life, motivations, and purpose. This takes you to the first step of the process of releasing fear which is to accept your fears and lacking. Remember, you cannot sort an issue if you deny that there isn't one.

Perfect Love is not dependent on relationships but rather refines and transforms you through its very experience. Those who have the courage to embrace this profound Love will face the reality of a Love that transcends childish, immature, and dependent ways of relating. It challenges you to let go of ego-driven control and surrender to the power of Love energy.

Experiencing this Love will slowly reshape and change you into the embodiment of the Love you have experienced. It is a journey that some may fear, as it requires surrendering the grip of the ego on your life. However, by embracing the power of Love energy, you can unlock a higher level of personal growth and fulfillment, free from the constraints of fear and control.

The All-Forgiving Love

Another powerful aspect of Love is forgiveness. Forgiveness serves the purpose of restoring your awareness that you are all created in Love and that Love provides you with everything you need. Fear, on the other hand, creates the illusion of scarcity, convincing you that you will never have enough Love and that you are lacking. This fear of scarcity becomes the biggest obstacle to forgiveness.

To find true peace, you must embrace complete forgiveness. This happens when you remember that Love is the abundant source that fulfills all your needs. When you recognize this, forgiveness becomes easier because you can empathize with others, reflecting inner tranquility and unconditional Love, regardless of how they may have hurt you. In this state, you remember that genuine forgiveness already exists within Perfect Love. Forgiveness becomes a powerful tool for correcting your misconceptions, allowing you to see only the Love in others and yourself and nothing else.

Love is the ultimate key to understanding your connection with Perfect Love as beings created from "stardust." As you cultivate deep Love for one another, you develop a desire to fully know and accept each other, embracing both the good and the challenging aspects. You discover that Love can withstand any situation or difficulty. Your relationships become the platform where you can truly shine and express your best self. The profound mystery of spirituality lies in the fact that God desires intimate oneness with you, regardless of whether you are considered a saint or sinner, with the same unwavering Love and acceptance (Kelsey, 1976).

Embrace the transformative power of forgiveness and love in your life. Let go of scarcity and fear, and open yourself to the abundant Love that surrounds you. By cultivating empathy, forgiveness, and acceptance, you will experience the depth and beauty of unconditional Love, both within yourself and in your relationships. Embrace the journey of Love and forgiveness, and witness the profound healing and growth that unfold along the way.

Here is a quick activity for you to know your lackings when it comes to Love Energy so that you can be aware of them and begin to improve them.

Open up to 1 Corinthians Chapter 13, which is all about The Way of Love, and write down verses 4 to 7, which are the qualities of Perfect Love.

To demonstrate: *Love is patient and kind; Love does not envy or boast; it is not arrogant or rude. It does not insist on its own way; it is not irritable or resentful; it does not rejoice at wrongdoing but rejoices with the truth. Love bears all things, believes all things, hopes all things, and endures all things.*

Now replace the word Love with your name. Since I am Scott, my passage will look something like this:

Scott is patient and kind. Scott does not envy or boast; Scott is not arrogant or rude. Scott does not insist on his own way; he is not irritable or resentful. Scott does not rejoice at wrongdoing but rejoices with the truth. Scott bears all things, believes all things, hopes all things, and endures all things.

Engaging in this activity allows you to gain a deeper understanding of the qualities of Perfect Love and how they align with your own personal growth and development to cast out the fears. By replacing the word "love" with your own name, such as Scott in this example, you personalize and internalize these qualities, making them a part of your self-awareness journey. Are there areas where you excel and embody these qualities? Are there areas where you may find room for improvement?

As you traverse this path of self-discovery and self-love, you not only tap into the boundless reservoir of Love within yourself but also become a beacon of light and compassion, inspiring others to embark on their own journey of Love. Each step is taken, each interaction, and each moment becomes an opportunity to radiate Love, fostering unity, healing, and transformation in your world. With your empowered understanding of your inherent connection to Perfect Love, you become an embodiment of Love's transformative power, enriching both your own life and the lives of those around you.

Chapter 8: Conscious Breathing and Love Energy Make You More......

In the hustle and bustle of your modern life, you may often find yourself caught up in a whirlwind of responsibilities, stress, and distractions. You might be yearning for a sense of balance, inner peace, and a deeper connection to yourself and others. But amidst the chaos, it can be challenging to find the path that leads you to such a profound transformation.

In this chapter, I will walk you through the extraordinary power of conscious breathing and its ability to unlock dormant potentials within us and develop abilities that may not be possible otherwise. By exploring the harmonious fusion of conscious breathing and love energy, embark on a journey that not only enhances your well-being but also enriches the drapes of your life in ways you never thought possible because you may not have viewed the power of conscious breathing and Love energy in such a difference before.

Let's discuss the impacts of conscious breathing and love energy on you and your life. Conscious Breathing and Love Energy Makes You More......

Forgiving:

In the realm of love energy, forgiveness shines as a remarkable characteristic. It holds the power to restore our awareness of our inherent nature as beings created in love, where all our needs are abundantly provided. Forgiveness becomes the means to dispel the illusion and falsehood of scarcity that fear creates, leading us to believe that we are lacking (Schucman and Thetford, 1975). The fear rooted in scarcity becomes the greatest obstacle to forgiveness, hindering our path to peace.

True peace can only be attained through complete forgiveness. And complete forgiveness is achieved by remembering that love, in its perfection, fulfills all our needs. It is through this remembrance that we can extend forgiveness to ourselves and others effortlessly. With inner tranquility and unconditional love reflecting from within, we can empathize with others, regardless of how they may have offended us. In this state, forgiveness becomes natural and easy.

As we embrace forgiveness, we begin to recognize that genuine forgiveness already exists within the realm of perfect love. It serves as a means to correct our misconceptions and illusions. Through forgiveness, we open our eyes to see only love in others and ourselves, leaving no room for anything else (Jampolsky, 1979).

Mindful:

Conscious breathing serves as a profound tool for cultivating mindfulness, which in turn brings about a deep sense of calm and leads you to inner peace. When you engage in conscious breathing, you purposefully bring your attention to the present moment, immersing yourself fully in the experience of each breath.

Mindfulness, at its core, is the practice of non-judgmental awareness of the present moment. By consciously directing your focus to the breath, you anchor yourself in the here and now, allowing you to detach from the incessant stream of thoughts, worries, and distractions that often consume your mind. As you become more attuned to the rhythm of your breath, you create a space of stillness and silence within, which enables you to observe your thoughts and emotions without judgment.

In a 2019 study, researchers examined the effects of a 5-week yoga and mindfulness intervention program on individuals. The results revealed that those who participated in the program showed greater improvement in anxiety, depression, and sleep issues compared to the control group. Furthermore, the study highlighted the immediate calming impact of taking deep, tranquil breaths during times of stress. Engaging in these calming breaths appeared to foster a more mindful perspective on the stressor at hand and how one could effectively manage it.

The connection between conscious breathing and mindfulness is symbiotic. As you engage in conscious breathing, your attention naturally gravitates towards the sensations of the breath entering and leaving your body. This heightened awareness of the breath acts as an anchor, grounding you in the present moment. In turn, mindfulness supports the deepening of your conscious breathing practice by allowing you to observe the breath with a non-judgmental attitude, free from attachment or aversion.

The cultivation of mindfulness through conscious breathing brings about a profound sense of calm. As we immerse ourselves in the rhythmic flow of the breath, we begin to let go of the constant mental chatter that often generates stress, anxiety, and restlessness. The mind becomes still, and serene tranquility envelops our being. In this state, we are no longer pulled in different directions by past regrets or future worries. We are fully present, embracing the beauty and simplicity of the present moment.

With consistent practice, conscious breathing and mindfulness become powerful tools for accessing inner peace. As you continue to deepen your mindfulness practice, you develop an innate ability to observe your thoughts and emotions without judgment or attachment. You become aware of the transient nature of your experiences and recognize that your peace and well-being are not dependent on external circumstances but are rooted within you.

In this state of inner peace, you cultivate resilience, emotional balance, and a heightened capacity to navigate the challenges of life with grace and equanimity. You learn to respond to situations rather than react impulsively, and you cultivate a sense of compassion and understanding towards yourselves and others.

By consciously integrating conscious breathing and mindfulness into your daily lives, you embark on a transformative journey that leads you towards a more mindful, calm, and peaceful existence. It is through this powerful union that you discover the profound connection between your breath, your mind, and your inner peace—a connection that has the potential to enhance every aspect of your life and bring you closer to a state of profound well-being.

Resilient:

Conscious breathing can empower you to develop resilience, enabling you to cope effectively with challenges and bounce back from adversity. By integrating conscious breathing practices into your daily life, you can cultivate a state of balance, inner strength, and adaptability that enhances your resilience.

- **Regulating the Stress Response:**
  You have the ability to directly influence your autonomic nervous system, which governs your stress response, through conscious breathing. Slow and deep breathing activates the parasympathetic nervous system, triggering a relaxation response that counteracts the effects of the sympathetic nervous system responsible for the fight-or-flight response (Jerath et al.,

2015).[8] By consciously controlling your breath, you can regulate your physiological responses to stress, reducing anxiety, hypertension, and heart rate and promoting a calmer state of mind.

- **Emotional Regulation:**
Resilience entails effectively managing and regulating your emotions, particularly in challenging situations. Conscious breathing plays a vital role in emotional regulation by promoting self-awareness and mindfulness. Mindful breathing practices increase activity in brain regions associated with emotional regulation, such as the prefrontal cortex, while reducing activity in the amygdala, which is responsible for emotional reactivity (Anselm et al., 2016).[9] This equilibrium allows you to respond to stressful situations with greater composure and emotional stability.

- **Cognitive Flexibility:**
Resilience requires the ability to adapt and think flexibly, finding alternative solutions and perspectives when faced with adversity.

---

[8] Jerath, R., Edry, J. W., Barnes, V. A., & Jerath, V. (2015). Physiology of long pranayamic breathing: Neural respiratory elements may provide a mechanism that explains how slow deep breathing shifts the autonomic nervous system. *Medical Hypotheses, 84(2),* 87-90.

[9] Doll, A., Hölzel, B. K., Bratec, S. M., Boucard, C. C., Xie, X., Wohlschläger, A. M., & Sorg, C. (2016). Mindful attention to breath regulates emotions via increased amygdala–prefrontal cortex connectivity. *NeuroImage, 134,* 305–313. https://doi.org/10.1016/j.neuroimage.2016.03.041

Engaging in conscious breathing practices enhances cognitive flexibility. A study by Leandro et al. (2015) demonstrated that deep breathing exercises significantly improved cognitive flexibility and performance.[10] By incorporating conscious breathing, you can cultivate a calm and focused state of mind that supports creative problem-solving and the ability to shift perspectives.

- **Building Mind-Body Awareness:**
Conscious breathing practices involve directing your attention to the sensations of your breath and body. Through heightened awareness, you develop a deeper connection with your body, gaining insight into your physical and emotional states. This mind-body awareness is a crucial component of resilience as it allows you to recognize and respond to stress signals before they escalate. By being attuned to your body, you can implement self-care strategies, seek support, and make proactive choices that promote well-being.

- **Enhancing Psychological Well-being:**
Resilience is closely intertwined with psychological well-being. Numerous studies

---

[10] Ferreira, L., Tanaka, K., Santos-Galduróz, R. F., & Galduróz, J. C. (2015). Respiratory training as a strategy to prevent cognitive decline in aging: a randomized controlled trial. *Clinical interventions in aging*, *10*, 593–603. https://doi.org/10.2147/CIA.S79560

have shown that conscious breathing practices, such as pranayama in yoga, mindfulness meditation, or focused breathing techniques, have positive effects on mental health outcomes. These practices have been found to reduce symptoms of anxiety, depression, and stress (Janet et al., 2017).[11] By improving your psychological well-being, conscious breathing creates a solid foundation for building resilience.

Confident:

Conscious breathing can indeed contribute to enhancing your confidence, empowering you to overcome challenges with a greater sense of self-assurance. By incorporating specific techniques and practices, you can harness the power of conscious breathing to boost your confidence levels and face obstacles with resilience and belief in your abilities.

- **Grounding and Centering:** One technique that can help is grounding and centering. By focusing on deep and intentional breaths, you can calm your mind, release tension, and center your attention on the task at hand. This grounding effect creates a solid foundation from which confidence can arise.

---

[11] McConville, J., McAleer, R., & Hahne, A. (2017). Mindfulness Training for Health Profession Students—The Effect of Mindfulness Training on Psychological Well-Being, Learning and Clinical Performance of Health Professional Students: A Systematic Review of Randomized and Non-randomized Controlled Trials. *EXPLORE, 13(1),* 26-45.

- **Body-Mind Connection:** You can also benefit from the body-mind connection that conscious breathing facilitates. By directing your attention to the breath and bodily sensations, you become more attuned to your physical presence, gaining a sense of embodiment and self-awareness. This heightened body-mind connection fosters a sense of confidence as you feel more connected to your strengths, capabilities, and inner resources.

- **Regulating Emotions:** When negative emotions such as fear, anxiety, or self-doubt undermine your confidence, conscious breathing practices can aid in emotional regulation. By consciously slowing down and deepening your breath, you activate the parasympathetic nervous system, triggering a relaxation response and reducing the intensity of emotional reactivity. This regulation of emotions creates space for more positive and empowering states of mind, enhancing your confidence.

- **Positive Self-Talk:** Combine conscious breathing with positive self-talk to reinforce a confident mindset. As you engage in slow and intentional breaths, simultaneously affirm positive statements or mantras that enhance your self-belief. By repeatedly affirming statements such as "I am capable," "I trust myself," or "I embrace challenges," you can strengthen your inner confidence and overcome self-limiting beliefs.

- **Visualization and Breathwork:** Utilize visualization techniques in conjunction with conscious breathing to build confidence. Imagine yourself successfully navigating challenging situations, visualizing yourself performing at your best and achieving your goals. Synchronize these visualizations with deep and focused breaths to condition your mind and body to associate confidence with the act of breathing, creating a positive feedback loop that reinforces a confident state.

By incorporating these techniques into your daily life, you can develop a more confident mindset and approach challenges with a greater sense of self-assurance. Conscious breathing serves as a powerful tool for cultivating confidence, grounding you in the present moment, enhancing your body-mind connection, and regulating your emotions, and it can be combined with positive self-talk and visualization. With consistent practice, conscious breathing can become a reliable ally in overcoming challenges and fostering unwavering confidence.

Kind:

Conscious breathing has the potential to improve your relationships with kindness. By practicing specific techniques and incorporating conscious breathing into your interactions, you can cultivate a sense of compassion, empathy, and connection.

- **Enhanced Presence and Active Listening:** When you engage in conscious breathing, you become more present in the moment. This presence allows you to truly listen to others, giving them your full attention and showing genuine interest in what they have to say. By being fully present and actively listening, you create a friendly and welcoming space for meaningful conversations and connections to occur.
- **Reduced Stress and Emotional Reactivity:** Conscious breathing helps regulate your stress response and promotes emotional balance. By taking deep, intentional breaths, you activate the relaxation response and calm your nervous system. This state of calmness allows you to respond to others with greater patience, understanding, and compassion rather than reacting impulsively or defensively. By managing your own emotions, you create a more kind and supportive atmosphere in your relationships.
- **Empathy and Understanding:** Conscious breathing practices can deepen your capacity for empathy and understanding.[12] By becoming more attuned to your own thoughts, feelings, and sensations through conscious breathing, you develop a

---

[12] O'Hanrahan, P. (n.d.). Conscious Breathing Practices for the Nine Types. The Enneagram at Work. Retrieved from https://theenneagramatwork.com/conscious-breathing-practices

heightened awareness of your own experiences. This increased self-awareness translates into a greater ability to empathize with others, as you can better recognize and connect with their emotions and perspectives. This empathetic understanding fosters loving kindness and strengthens interpersonal bonds.

- **Non-judgmental Attitude:** Conscious breathing encourages a non-judgmental attitude towards yourself and others. As you focus on the breath and cultivate a state of mindfulness, you learn to observe thoughts and emotions without attaching judgments or labels. This non-judgmental mindset extends to your interactions with others, allowing you to approach them with acceptance and openness. By embracing a non-judgmental attitude, you create an environment of friendliness and inclusivity.

- **Conflict Resolution and Emotional Regulation:** Conscious breathing can be a powerful tool in conflict resolution and emotional regulation within relationships.[13] When faced with conflicts or disagreements, taking conscious breaths can help you stay calm, centered, and composed. This centered

---

[13] Higgins, G. (2019, October 3). Mindfulness can be a powerful conflict-resolution tool. People Management. Retrieved from https://www.peoplemanagement.co.uk/article/1741633/mindfulness-as-a-powerful-conflict-resolution-tool

state enables you to respond to conflicts in a more constructive and friendly manner, promoting understanding, compromise, and effective communication. By regulating your own emotions through conscious breathing, you contribute to a more harmonious and friendly dynamic in your relationships.

- **Mindful Communication:** Mindful breathing underpins deliberate communication, encompassing sincere self-expression and attentive listening. Integrating conscious breathing into your communication cultivates heightened awareness of your language, tone, and nonverbal cues. This heightened awareness facilitates communication characterized by respect, kindness, and amiability. Mindful communication establishes affirmative bonds and elevates relationship caliber.

Incorporating conscious breathing into your daily life can contribute to your overall loving kindness and improve your relationships. By cultivating presence, reducing stress and emotional reactivity, fostering empathy and understanding, adopting a non-judgmental attitude, promoting conflict resolution and emotional regulation, and practicing mindful communication, conscious breathing helps you develop friendlier interactions and build stronger connections with others.

Creative:

Conscious breathing can indeed enhance your creativity, providing you with a pathway for unlocking innovative thinking and tapping into your artistic potential. By incorporating specific conscious breathing techniques and practices, you can cultivate a more creative mindset and experience a flow of ideas that lead to original and imaginative outcomes.

- **Stress Reduction and Mental Clarity:** When you engage in slow and intentional breaths, you activate your parasympathetic nervous system, which triggers a relaxation response. This reduces stress and promotes mental clarity, allowing your mind to let go of distractions and worries. By reducing stress and mental clutter, conscious breathing enables you to approach challenges with a clearer and more focused mind, facilitating creative problem-solving.

- **Enhanced Brain Function:** Research has shown that conscious breathing practices can enhance brain function and cognition. Deep and rhythmic breathing increases the supply of oxygen to your brain, which is essential for optimal cognitive performance. Additionally, conscious breathing activates the default mode network (DMN), a brain network associated with creativity and self-referential thinking. By stimulating the DMN through conscious breathing, you can access a state of mind conducive to generating innovative ideas.

- **Mindfulness and Sensory Awareness:** Conscious breathing is often accompanied by mindfulness practices, which involve bringing your attention to the present moment without judgment. Through mindfulness, you become more aware of your sensory experiences and thoughts, fostering a deeper connection with your surroundings and inner self. This heightened sensory awareness can serve as a rich source of inspiration for your creative endeavors as you become more attuned to your emotions, sensations, and surroundings, influencing your creative expression.

- **Embracing the "Flow" State:** Conscious breathing can facilitate the experience of "flow," a state of optimal performance and complete absorption in an activity. By calming your mind and creating a conducive environment for deep focus and creativity, conscious breathing helps you enter the flow state. In this state, creative ideas flow effortlessly, and you feel inspired and in tune with your creative impulses.

- **Promoting Divergent Thinking:** Divergent thinking, which involves generating multiple solutions and ideas, is critical for creativity. Conscious breathing supports divergent thinking by increasing cognitive flexibility and promoting a more open and expansive mindset. By consciously regulating your breath, you can break free from mental constraints and explore a wide range of possibilities, leading to more innovative and original ideas.

- **Connecting with Intuition:** Conscious breathing practices encourage you to tap into your intuition and inner wisdom. By quieting your mind and becoming more present, you can access deeper insights and ideas that may not be immediately apparent through analytical thinking. Intuition plays a significant role in creative breakthroughs and originality, and conscious breathing provides a pathway for connecting with this valuable resource.

It is overwhelming to realize the potential of conscious breathing to profoundly impact various aspects of your life, making you more mindful, calm, resilient, confident, kind and creative. By incorporating this magical act into your life, you sign up for countless benefits. You can harness the power of conscious breathing to cultivate these qualities and enhance your overall well-being.

It is a lifelong journey of self-discovery and self-mastery. As you commit to this practice, embrace the transformative power of conscious breathing and experience the profound impact it can have on your well-being, relationships, and creative pursuits. May you continue to breathe consciously, cultivate mindfulness, and nurture your inner self as you navigate the beautiful tapestry of life.

Chapter 9: Divine Truth and Spiritual Empowerment

In your life, many of your memories and experiences may be accompanied by emotional or physical pain and cognitive distortion. The extent of this pain and distortion can create barriers within your mind and body, limiting your ability to fully embrace the transformative power of Love Energy and enlighten yourself with the Divine Truth. Hidden hurts, unmet needs, and repressed emotions might be holding you back from accessing the Truth that has the potential to set you free.

In your present life, various aspects such as relationships, behaviors, perceptions, and your overall personality can be influenced by the projection of a memory picture, matching emotion, and the embedded original lie. These elements from the past often find their way into your current experiences. It's important to understand that memories come in different forms: visual, emotional/feeling, and physical. Each of these memories carries an embedded original lie, as noted by Smith (1996). It's not only your present circumstances that contribute to your pain; they can also act as triggers, opening the window to painful experiences and distortions from the past. Over time, layers of lies become intertwined with each successive life event connected to the original painful and distorted memory.

Types of cognitive distortion:

In your journey of self-discovery, it is important to understand the three types of cognitive distortion, or lies, that can impact your perception and beliefs:

1. **Metamorphic lies** are those that were true when the original event occurred but are no longer true in your present reality. For example, a near-fatal accident or illness might have led you to believe, "I am going to die." However, in your current circumstances, this belief is no longer valid or accurate.

2. **The cluster lies** involve multiple lies that stem from a single original event, each carrying its own intensity. For instance, you might hold beliefs such as "I am dumb, I am helpless, I am unworthy," all associated with the same event. These cluster lies can create a complex web of negative thoughts and perceptions about yourself.

3. **Cloned lies** encompass multiple individual events, each reinforcing the same lie. For instance, you may have experienced different life events, but the underlying belief that "I am a failure" remains constant. Each experience becomes another piece of evidence that seemingly supports this distorted belief.

In your journey of self-discovery, it is essential to understand the various emotions that are commonly associated with cognitive distortions and these lies. According to Smith (1996), eight emotions are frequently intertwined with these distortions: fear, abandonment, shame, tainted, confusion, hopelessness, invalidation, and powerlessness. It is important to note that while these emotions may not originate from lies themselves, they often have connections to experiences of grief and loss.

These emotions, stemming from past experiences, can become entangled with cognitive distortions, shaping your beliefs and perceptions of yourself and the world. Childhood experiences, societal influences, and even misguided teachings can contribute to the development of these distortions and emotions. For example, one of the fundamental lies that you often learn in childhood is that you must judge your behavior, conduct, and performance before God, prioritizing them over your relationship with God/Love (Seamands, 1985). Many adults who seek inner peace and aim to please God may find themselves caught in a never-ending cycle of trying to please God with actions instead of focusing on establishing a personal relationship with Him. They may believe that by reading another chapter, praying for another hour, or taking on additional responsibilities at church, they will finally find the peace they seek. Unfortunately, that is not the case. True inner peace and a genuine connection with God are not achieved through these external acts alone. It is crucial to understand that these actions, while valuable, should not overshadow the importance of nurturing your relationship with God.

During childhood, you learn vital concepts like Love, acceptance, faith, justice, and dependability based on real experiences, with your parents playing a profound role in shaping your understanding of Love. These early experiences become the foundation of your perception and experience of Love. While they may be doing it to the best of their knowledge, it is noteworthy to realize that they may not always be the accurate representation of the Divine Truth and God's Love.

Therefore to change your paradigms and make right your perceptions, it is important to release the emotional and physical intensity associated with painful memories and to diffuse their compulsive power by engaging in the practice of Breathing Love Energy with the Breathe Love Method. By intentionally directing love energy towards healing and aligning with Divine Truth, you can free yourself from the grip of these painful memories (Seamands, 1991). Through this intentional practice, you can tap into the transformative power of love energy, allowing it to infuse your being and provide healing on both emotional and physical levels. The presence of Divine Truth is one of the most vital and remarkable elements of Breathing Love in your life. The pursuit of Divine Truth has long been a recognized goal of spiritual enlightenment. It is based on the belief that higher power, with a universal and cosmic understanding of human experience, exists beyond the illusions of everyday life. This belief serves as the foundation for personal growth and healing (Goldsmith, 1959).

Embrace the practice of Breathing Love Energy with the Breathe Love Method on a daily basis with the intention of healing and connecting with Divine Truth. By doing so, you open the doors to release the burdens of painful memories and experience a greater sense of freedom, emotional well-being, and inner peace. Remember that your journey is unique, and by cultivating a deeper connection with love energy and aligning with Divine Truth, you can find healing, liberation, and a renewed sense of purpose and joy in your life.

Spiritual enlightenment

Another natural aspect of your personal growth and healing involves the development of your personality, moving away from a childlike self-centered focus towards embracing the concept of others and making commitments to them. This evolutionary process transcends your own wants and desires, expanding to encompass a larger purpose where your individual needs are interconnected with a dependent relationship with everyone around you. This fundamental law of social reciprocity forms the bedrock of your spiritual identity, connecting you to a Higher Power that exists beyond and holds greater significance than your individual self.

The process of spiritual empowerment is facilitated by practicing Breathing Love, which can have a profound impact on your journey. Through Breathing Love, you open yourself to the presence and experience of Love itself. As Goldsmith (1959) suggests, prayer is a way to connect with the presence of God, and the practice of Breathing Love allows grace and self-forgiveness to transform you from within.

Grace, being conscious of Light and Divinity, is experienced through prayer and has a calming effect on your being. It becomes a cycle where grace brings tranquility to your soul, and in turn, you gain a deeper understanding that every experience you encounter is necessary for your growth. This knowing, instilled by grace, brings a sense of calm and assurance (Zukav, 1990). As you engage in the practice of Breathing Love, you not only touch your essential being, but you also recognize and awaken your personal spiritual power (Koch, 1998). This awakening propels you to take action, embrace personal growth, and reclaim the power of Love within yourself.

In your quest for meaning, purpose, and a deeper connection, it is essential to explore spirituality and its significance in your life (Koch, 1998). Here, the term "Higher Power" encompasses various concepts of universal Love Energy, such as Christ, Eastern beliefs like Buddhism, Hinduism, Islam, Native American beliefs, the Tao, or the universal notions of Love and Truth. Spirituality can be understood as any personal encounter with this universal Love and the application of that experience to your mind, body, and overall life journey. As noted by McCullough and Worthington (1995), your spirituality has the potential to shape how you observe and perceive events. It is considered a vital aspect of your humanity, intricately woven into your physical, psychological, and social dimensions.

In this journey of spirituality, it is important to acknowledge that it encompasses both the experience of Love and fear. Love, as defined by Peck (1978), is the will to extend oneself for the purpose of nurturing one's own or another's spiritual growth. This definition highlights the inherent desire for connection and growth that resides within each of us. Frankl (1984) adds to this understanding by emphasizing that the search for life's meaning naturally leads us to look beyond ourselves. This quest for meaning compels us to explore connections outside of ourselves, seeking relationships with others and a Higher Power (Love Energy). Adler (1950) further describes this interconnectedness as an innate desire for community, encompassing relationships with nature, others, and a Higher Power.

God/Love is the creator of all things. Spirituality, then, lies at the core of your humanness. It involves the process of becoming a person in the fullest sense (Marquarrie, 1972). It is through your spiritual journey that you tap into the depths of your being, embracing your capacity for Love, connection, and personal growth.

Developing a deeper connection with the Creator can also help strengthen the oneness of your mind, body, Spirit, and emotions. When your mind aligns with the Creative power of God/Love, you experience a profound sense of clarity and wisdom. You are guided towards divine intelligence, enabling you to make choices that are in alignment with your highest good. The Creator's wisdom illuminates your thoughts, helping you discern Truth from illusion and empowering you with Love and energy to live with authenticity and purpose.

Nurturing a connection with the Creative power of love energy also impacts your physical well-being, as discussed. Your body becomes a vessel through which divine love energy flows, revitalizing and healing you and others through you at a profound level. Jesus said to the Samaritan woman at the well, *"Jesus answered and said to her, "Everyone who drinks of this water will thirst again, but whoever drinks of the water that I will give him shall never thirst; but the water that I will give him will become in him a well of water springing up to eternal life."* (John 4:5-30) It is widely recognized that in the ancient languages, the word "water" was a metaphor for our emotions._When Creative Love Energy resides in your heart, a profound transformation takes place, renewing every aspect of your being.

By embracing God/Love and honoring your body as a sacred temple of the Spirit, you create a harmonious connection, a sacred bond that encourages the cultivation of habits and practices to promote your overall health, vitality, and balance. The Creative power of divine love infuses your physical being, providing unwavering support on your path toward holistic well-being. And as you progress and discover the hidden gems, you realize that it is not an easy path and the journey of search of divine Truth while constantly staying in connection with the love energy requires patience and consistency, but the reward is worth striving for.

In your journey, your mind and body become the instruments through which you seek Divine Truth. As you align with this Truth, it governs all aspects of your mind and body, equipping you with the capacity to access the knowledge you need. Simply setting your intention to invite the presence of universal Love into your life opens the path for Divine Truth to reveal itself to you. Through this powerful combination of Truth and Love Energy, you will witness the emergence of new insights and memories that are free from human illusions. Your mind will be liberated to remember deeply repressed and distorted events (Seamands, 1985).

Recognize that unresolved aspects within you might hinder the profound healing and growth offered by Love Energy. However, you possess the power to overcome these barriers. By embracing the Divine Truth through the practice of Breathing Love, you unlock the potential for transformative personal change. This journey of self-discovery empowers you to transcend past limitations and gain clarity in the present, enabling you to confidently move forward in your life's journey. Through nurturing your bond with Universal Love and letting Truth illuminate your path, you'll encounter healing, growth, and an enriched comprehension of your innate divine essence.

To truly embrace spirituality and empowerment, it is essential to transcend the limitations of the mind and body and explore the expansive nature of the "self." Empowerment arises from actively exercising your free will to choose a higher, more Perfect Love and Truth that can only be found through connection with the universal God spirit. Zukav (1990) describes this evolved state of self as a "multisensory person" who recognizes that the five sensory experience of life is no longer sufficient. They intentionally seek experiences beyond the physical realm, delving into an "invisible realm" where their deepest values and truths are discovered. Dossey (1989) refers to this state as the nonlocal mind, a space where the true essence of the soul resides.

In this invisible realm, the energy of the soul is recognized, valued and begins to merge with your personality, resulting in what is known as "authentic empowerment." It is the alignment of your personality, rooted in the five sensory experiences, with the powerful and positive source at the core of your being – the soul.

Zukav further explains that the journey from being un-empowered to becoming empowered is a process of evolution. As an empowered individual, you have the ability to choose a reverent and spiritual path, embracing qualities like patience and peace. This involves a willingness to delay the gratification of your five sensory needs and perceptions.

In your empowered state, you can examine your feelings, perceptions, values, and behaviors through the lens of achieving wholeness. By gaining a deeper understanding of your struggles with power and how they impact your connection to your true soul, you can foster personal growth and fulfillment.

On the other hand, an unempowered person may find it difficult to fulfill the desires of their soul. They often seek external power, overachieve, and seek immediate gratification based on fear. Unfortunately, this pursuit can leave them feeling empty and dissatisfied. They may focus their attention on the faults and shortcomings of others, which only elicits disdain, anger, and hatred in return. Moreover, it is important to recognize that seeking to dominate others ultimately leads to self-disempowerment. The more we try to control that which is external, the less empowered we feel. In contrast, an empowered individual seeks to nurture rather than control and aims to empower rather than dominate.

Humbleness, forgiveness, clarity, and Love serve as the key dynamics of empowerment in your life. They provide you with a clear choice between learning through Love and Truth or learning through doubt and fear. Foster (1983) offers insights into the process of spiritual empowerment, describing it as a meditative prayer where you go beyond mere mental engagement. By bringing your mind into your heart, your soul awakens, allowing you to listen with your entire being. This deep listening connects you to the profound wisdom that resides within you. Furthermore, Kelsey (1976) highlights the spiritual witness and insight of the saints, who have experienced God in moments of solitude and internal stillness. It is important to recognize that you need not become a monk to have similar experiences. As an ordinary person, you have the capacity to turn inward, allowing yourself to be touched by the transformative power of Love energy. In these moments of connection, you are able to undergo personal transformation and experience renewal.

It is important for you to accept that experiencing Love energy is often easier than fully understanding it (Chambers, 1962). To cultivate a deeper connection with the Love within your soul, consider establishing a ritual or practice of solitude and inner silence (Myss, 1997) that my Breathe Love Method can provide. Through this intentional practice, you create a space that allows you to remember and connect with the profound Love that resides within you. As you develop in the practice of being in the presence of Love, you will begin to experience realizations and insights. These realizations are followed by tangible demonstrations of Love in your life (Goldsmith, 1959). It is in this state of being, immersed in the presence of Love, that you will find true freedom and empowerment.

In your pursuit of spiritual empowerment, it is important to understand the two-part process described by Koch (1998), inspired by the teachings of Joseph Campbell, a renowned figure in spiritual counseling.

- **Firstly,** spiritual empowerment begins with an experience of connecting to a Higher Power. This spiritual connection opens the door to a deeper understanding of your own spiritual power.

- **Secondly,** the process involves accepting and awakening to your inherent spiritual power and finding the courage to utilize it. Through this process, you will experience a greater sense of spiritual empowerment, which fuels your desire for an ongoing connection with the Higher Power, leading to a continuously expanding spiral of spiritual power.

To fully embrace your spiritual power, it is crucial to make conscious choices and exercise your free will. Embrace spiritual principles such as forgiveness, surrender, prayer, meditation, worship, and service (Koch, 1998). By actively engaging in these practices, you will begin to recognize and unfold your spiritual power, further intensifying your desire for greater spiritual potential. As you embrace and utilize your spiritual power, the influence of material concerns, daily hassles, and the control exerted by others gradually diminishes. The result of spiritual empowerment is a greater sense of oneness and connection with others. Through your journey of spiritual empowerment, you will find a deep sense of interconnectedness, expanding your capacity for compassion, understanding, and Love.

The Concept of Oneness:

Goldsmith (1959) beautifully describes oneness as a spiritual and invisible force that underlies all of creation. If we consider this force to be God, then everything we inherit stems from the divine source, the Mother-Father-God. It is an emanation of one Life, expressing, revealing, demonstrating, and manifesting itself individually, universally, impersonally, and impartially. It is important to remember that there is no separation between your personality and your soul (Scolastico, 1995). McLaren (1994) emphasizes that our failure to see our reflection in others diminishes the potential for self and social change, ultimately causing us to disconnect from our own Spirit.

Embracing the concept of oneness allows you to recognize the interconnectedness of all beings and the divine essence that flows through each of us. By acknowledging the reflection of yourself in others, you deepen your understanding of unity and nurture a sense of shared humanity. You are an integral part of the divine tapestry of life. Embrace the interconnected nature of existence, recognizing that your actions, thoughts, and intentions have a ripple effect on the world around you. By cultivating a sense of oneness, you contribute to the collective growth and transformation of both yourself and society.

Using the Breathe Love Method, you can tap into the limitless well of Love, compassion, and wisdom that resides within you. Embrace the Truth of oneness, and let it guide your interactions, choices, and the way you navigate the world. As you deepen your connection to oneness, you will experience a profound and never-ending sense of unity, purpose, and fulfillment.

Chapter 10: Bringing it All Together

Welcome to the final chapter of this journey—a journey that has unveiled the profound practice of Consciously Breathing Love through the Breath Love Method to harness your mental and physical well-being. Throughout this book, you explored the universal art of conscious breathing, a practice that unites people of diverse backgrounds, going beyond religion and culture. Now, as you approach the end of this exploration, you stand at the threshold of fully embracing the potential of Breathing Love.

This chapter marks the conclusion of the guidance, practices, experiences, reflections, and discoveries you have made along the path of conscious breathing and embracing Love energy to enhance the quality of your life and health. It is aimed at concluding this guidance into a lifestyle for you to adopt in your daily lives with full awareness of what you are practicing, why you are practicing, and how to monitor the results of the hard work that you do. It is the understanding of love that resides within every breath and the deep connection with the divine that awaits you to transform you when you simply become present with yourselves. Love and Consciousness is the key to every breath you breathe to make this connection stronger, fostering your well-being.

From ancient Eastern mystics to modern Western practitioners, you witnessed how breath practices have been a gateway to inner peace, healing, and empowerment, bridging the gap between you and the divine. You delved into the significance of conscious breathing in various spiritual traditions, discovering the common threads that bind you all.

Throughout this book, you were walked through the importance of personal experience and practice as a source of affirmation and truth, and in this chapter, you will also hear the stories and testimonies of those who have ventured into the realms of conscious breathing and love energy only to find its amazing benefits. They'll recount their transformations, liberations, and encounters with profound love within themselves and the world around them. The time has come to incorporate the step-by-step process in your life that will guide you toward a fulfilling conscious breathing practice. Get ready to set sail and embrace positive change and growth in your life. Let's explore the path that awaits you on this transformative regime.

Understanding Goals for Conscious Breathing Regime:

Setting clear goals is like embarking on a voyage with a well-charted map. Imagine you are the captain of a ship, and your destination is a distant, unexplored island. Without a clear goal and a map to guide you, you would be adrift in the vast ocean, unsure of where you are headed. However, with a detailed map and a clear destination in mind, you can navigate through storms, adjust your course when needed, and stay focused on reaching your desired island. Similarly, in establishing a dedicated, conscious breathing regime, setting clear goals provides you with direction, purpose, and motivation. By setting clear goals and cultivating regular practice, you can harness the transformative power of each breath. Let's explore the steps to help you navigate this rewarding voyage of conscious breathing:

1. **Start with Clarity:** Begin your conscious breathing journey by gaining a clear understanding of your intentions and desired outcomes. Take some time to reflect on what you hope to achieve through conscious breathing. Whether your goal is to reduce stress, improve focus, or enhance overall well-being, having a clear purpose will provide direction to your practice.

2. **Be Realistic:** While setting goals, it's essential to be realistic and practical. Start with smaller, attainable targets that you can comfortably achieve. Avoid overwhelming yourself with overly ambitious objectives. By starting with manageable goals, you can maintain motivation and build confidence as you progress.

3. **Create a Structured Plan:** Outline a structured plan for your conscious breathing practice. Define the frequency and duration of your sessions. For instance, you might begin with short sessions of 5 to 10 minutes and gradually increase the duration as you become more comfortable with the practice. Having a well-defined plan will help you stay on track and measure your progress.

4. **Choose Suitable Techniques:** Explore different breathing techniques that align with your specific

goals. For relaxation, consider trying diaphragmatic breathing, a technique that promotes calmness and reduces stress. If your aim is to improve focus, experiment with box breathing or alternate nostril breathing, which can enhance concentration and mindfulness. Select the techniques that resonate best with you and your objectives.

5. **Establish a Consistent Routine:** Consistency is key to making conscious breathing an integral part of your daily life. Set specific times for your practice and try to adhere to them as closely as possible. Integrating conscious breathing into your daily routine will reinforce the habit and ensure that you benefit from it regularly. Whether it's during your morning routine, before meals, or before bedtime, find a schedule that works for you and stick to it.

By understanding your goals, being realistic in your approach, creating a well-structured plan, choosing suitable techniques, and establishing a consistent routine, you will lay a strong foundation for a successful conscious breathing practice. With dedication and persistence, you can unlock the full potential of this practice and experience its profound positive effects on your well-being.

How to Incorporate Conscious Breathing into Daily Life

The essence of Breathing Love is a universal practice, accessible to all seeking a deeper connection with the divine. It transcends religious barriers and invites you to embrace love, compassion, and understanding as guiding principles on your spiritual path. Take this last step of your journey, breathing in the essence of love, discovering the divinity within, and letting the truth of Breathing Love set you free by religiously incorporating Conscious Breathing into your daily life. It is a powerful and transformative practice that can lead you toward greater spiritual empowerment and inner peace. As you embark on this journey, keep in mind the following guidance to make the most of this practice:

1. **Begin with Awareness:** Start by bringing your attention to your breath. Observe the natural rhythm of your breath without trying to change it. Allow yourself to fully experience each inhalation and exhalation, anchoring yourself in the present moment.

2. **Deepen the Breath:** Slowly deepen your breath, inhaling deeply through your nose and exhaling fully through your mouth. As you do this, let go of any tension or stress you may be carrying within you. Remember this circular breathing

3. **Embrace Mindfulness:** As you continue to breathe consciously, let go of any distracting thoughts or worries. Be fully present with each breath, letting go of the past and releasing any attachment to the future.

4. **Practice Gratitude:** Use Conscious Breathing as a time to express gratitude for the blessings in your life. With each inhalation, draw in feelings of gratitude and love, and with each exhalation, release any negativity or self-doubt.

5. **Set Intentions:** As you breathe consciously, set intentions for the day ahead or for any specific challenges you may be facing. Visualize yourself

overcoming obstacles and embracing opportunities for growth and empowerment. Though the benefits of Conscious breathing are free from the bondage of time, yet it is advisable to begin your day with a session of it.

For example: I intended to approach my work with confidence and creativity, tackling any obstacles with a clear and focused mind. I visualized myself presenting my ideas with passion and clarity, knowing that I had valuable contributions to make. And in my personal life, I set an intention to be more patient and compassionate with my loved ones. I wanted to respond to situations with love and understanding, fostering deeper connections in my relationships.

6. **Incorporate Breathing Breaks:** Throughout the day, take short breaks to reconnect with Conscious Breathing and breathe in Love Energy. Even a few moments of focused breathing can help you find calmness and clarity amidst a busy schedule.

7. **Be Patient with Yourself:** Remember that developing a regular Conscious Breathing practice takes time and patience. Be gentle with yourself and allow the process to unfold naturally.

8. **Journal Your Insights:** Keep a journal to record your experiences and insights during your Conscious Breathing practice. This will help you track your progress and reflect on the transformative changes taking place within you.

For example: I decided to try conscious breathing for the first time today. Finding a quiet spot, I sat down and closed my eyes. At first, my mind was restless, but I focused on my breath. Inhale, exhale. I felt a sense of calm washing over me. My mind kept wandering to random thoughts, but I gently brought my focus back each time. As I continued, my breath became deeper, and I felt more present in the moment. By the end of the practice, something incredible happened. I felt more relaxed, and my mind was clearer. It was like a weight had been lifted off my shoulders. I experienced a profound sense of peace and contentment that I hadn't felt in a long time. I decided to keep a journal to record these insights and track my progress on this transformative journey of conscious breathing.

9. **Embrace Compassion:** As you deepen your connection with yourself through Conscious Breathing, extend that same compassion and love to others. Embrace the oneness of all beings, recognizing the interconnectedness of humanity.

This simple yet thoughtful practice can guide you toward a life filled with love, peace, and purpose. As you breathe consciously, you align with the universal Love Energy and unlock the potential for growth and connection within yourself and the world around you. Embrace this journey of self-discovery and empowerment, and let the power of Conscious Breathing lead you towards a life of health with minimum to zero health risks.

Tips for maintaining a regular conscious breathing practice:

Remember that maintaining a regular conscious breathing regime can greatly enhance your physical, mental, and spiritual well-being. Drawing from the knowledge and insights shared in this chat, here are some tips to help establish and sustain a mindful breath practice:

1. **Set a Daily Routine:** Like any other habit, consistency is key to making conscious breathing a part of your daily life. Set aside a specific time each day for your breath practice, whether it's in the morning, during lunch, or before bedtime.

2. **Start with Short Sessions:** If you are new to conscious breathing, begin with short sessions of 5-10 minutes and gradually increase the duration as you become more comfortable with the practice.

3. **Create a Sacred Space**: Designate a quiet and peaceful space for your breath practice. This can be a corner of a room, a cozy nook, or any place where you feel comfortable and undisturbed.

4. **Posture and Comfort**: Find a comfortable sitting position with your back straight. You can sit cross-legged on a cushion, on a chair, or even lie down if that feels more relaxing. Good posture will keep you away from any kind of ache that you might experience, keeping you motivated to continue breathing Love.

5. **Focus on Your Breath:** Observe your breath without trying to control it. Pay attention to the

sensations of the air entering and leaving your body, the rise and fall of your chest or abdomen, and the rhythm of your breath.

6. **Counting Breath**: To stay focused, you can try counting your breaths. Inhale slowly to a count of four, hold for two, and exhale to a count of six. This simple technique can help regulate your breath and calm your mind.

7. **Use Mantras or Affirmations:** Incorporate mantras or affirmations that resonate with you into your breath practice. For example, silently repeat "peace," "love," or "let go" on each inhale and exhale.

8. **Mindful Breathing in Daily Activities:** Extend your conscious breathing beyond formal sessions. Practice mindfulness during daily activities like walking, eating, or waiting in line by simply being aware of your breath.

9. **Utilize Guided Meditation:** Guided meditation sessions are structured meditation practices led by experienced guides, teachers, or meditation instructors. During these sessions, the guide provides verbal instructions and prompts to help participants relax, focus their minds, and engage in specific meditation techniques. You may utilize guided meditation sessions or even breathwork apps that can help you stay on track and explore different breathing techniques.

10. **Join a Community or Class:** Consider joining a local breathwork or meditation group or attending workshops. Connecting with others on the same journey can provide support and motivation.

11. **Notice the Benefits:** Take note of the positive impacts that conscious breathing brings to your daily life. As you practice regularly, you may notice improvements such as increased focus, reduced stress, emotional balance, and greater mental clarity. These benefits are some of the rewards you can experience through conscious breathing.

However, if you find that you are not observing these benefits in your daily life, it might be a good idea to reflect on what could be hindering your progress or what areas you could work on to enhance your practice. Remember that each individual's journey is unique, and adjustments and improvements are always possible to deepen your experience with conscious breathing.

Measuring Progress in Your Conscious Breathing Practice

Measuring progress in conscious breathing is akin to taking stock of a flourishing garden. Just as a gardener regularly assesses the growth of plants and flowers, tracking your progress in conscious breathing allows you to nurture your inner garden of well-being. Similar to tending to the garden with care, measuring progress in conscious breathing empowers you to cultivate your practice with intention and mindfulness. By setting specific goals, you plant the seeds of positive change and guide your efforts toward achieving the desired outcomes.

As a gardener observes how each plant responds to sunlight, water, and nourishment, tracking progress in conscious breathing reveals how this practice positively influences your daily life. You become attuned to the moments of increased calmness, enhanced focus, and improved emotional regulation, just as a gardener witnesses the blossoming of flowers under careful attention. Moreover, just as the garden's growth can be subtle and gradual, measuring progress in conscious breathing helps you appreciate the incremental changes within yourself. Each day of dedicated practice contributes to a more profound sense of well-being, much like how consistent care for the garden yields a bountiful harvest over time.

Similar to adjusting the gardening techniques based on observations, tracking progress in conscious breathing allows you to make informed adjustments in your practice. Whether you note areas of improvement or identify challenges, this self-awareness empowers you to adapt and refine your approach, ensuring optimal growth and development. Here are a few methods to monitor your development and success:

1. **Keeping a Journal:** Maintain a journal to record your experiences, insights, and any changes you notice during and after each conscious breathing session. Write down your feelings, thoughts, and any emotions that arise during the practice. For example, you may note feeling more relaxed and focused after a morning breathing session or how conscious breathing helped you handle a stressful situation with greater ease during the day.

2. **Observing Daily Life:** Pay close attention to how conscious breathing impacts your daily life. Notice if you feel calmer and more centered in challenging situations. Observe whether you experience

improved focus and productivity at work or in your studies. These real-life improvements serve as tangible indicators of your progress in the practice.

3. **Utilizing Biofeedback Devices:** While not necessary, wearable biofeedback devices can offer objective data to gauge your progress. These devices can measure metrics like heart rate, breathing rate, and stress levels. For instance, you might notice a gradual decrease in your heart rate during and after conscious breathing sessions, indicating a heightened state of relaxation and calmness.

4. **Engaging in Self-Reflection:** Take time to reflect on your conscious breathing journey periodically. Assess whether you are achieving the goals you initially set and if there are areas you'd like to improve. Self-awareness will enable you to make necessary adjustments and stay on track with your practice. For example, you may realize that you tend to experience more benefits from conscious breathing when you practice in a quiet, secluded space and use this insight to create a more conducive environment for your sessions.

5. **Seeking Feedback:** If you have a meditation or breathing teacher, consider seeking their feedback on your progress. They can offer valuable insights, guidance, and personalized tips to enhance your conscious breathing practice. Their expertise can help you refine your techniques and deepen your understanding of the practice.

Remember that progress in conscious breathing may not always follow a linear path. Some days you might experience significant breakthroughs, while others may feel more subtle. Embrace the journey, be patient with yourself, and celebrate every step, no matter how small, as you continue to Breathe Love. Celebrate each milestone, no matter how humble, and let them be your guiding stars as you traverse the uncharted realms of conscious living. Your conscious breathing practice is a vessel for self-discovery, self-compassion, and self-awareness, enabling you to navigate life's currents with a steady hand and an open heart.

Testimonies

~ **Ivan**: *I encountered Dr. Ragsdale during a period of profound darkness in my life. His guidance marked the inception of a transformative journey encompassing mental, physical, and spiritual healing. This journey has accompanied me over the past 7 ½ years. Under Dr. Ragsdale's expert tutelage, I not only rekindled self-love but also embarked on a voyage of healing, self-realization, and inner tranquility. By sharing my narrative, I aspire to lend a helping hand to those who may harbor reservations about embracing Dr. Scott Ragsdale's holistic approach to healing and self-discovery. My personal odyssey, guided by his expertise, became my salvation, and I earnestly wish it to become yours as well.*

****

~ **David C.** *During my first BreathPrayerTM session, something truly remarkable occurred. I found myself having a vivid experience of being in the presence of God, and I could actually feel God's arms gently enveloping me. This was a revelation for me, especially considering that I had grown up as a minister's son and had been part of church life for as long as I could remember. Yet, nothing had prepared me for an encounter like this. Recounting the experience, I shared, "It was the most reassuring and tranquil feeling I've ever experienced in my entire life."*

Interestingly, during that initial session, I also managed to release a significant amount of pent-up anger that had been dwelling within me. As I continued with subsequent

BreathPrayerTM sessions, I began to receive insights into the underlying fears that were fueling that anger. Among these fears, one stood out: my apprehension regarding finances. Even though I had consistently provided for my family, I couldn't shake the constant worry that my source of income might vanish one day. I've always carried a sense of responsibility, but the weight of caring for my wife and children often felt overwhelming.

However, while practicing Breathing Love, a transformative realization began to take shape. It became clear that to truly love myself as Jesus had taught, I needed to safeguard my inner peace. This realization was instrumental in helping me overcome my fear of finances. From that point onward, whenever the fear resurfaced, I consciously entrusted it to God. Moreover, the divine truth that I embraced through BreathPrayerTMM taught me that my worth wasn't tied solely to my financial accomplishments. Instead, my true value lay in my capacity to extend love and compassion to those closest to me, as well as to every individual I encountered in life.

I also came to recognize that my anger, the need to control people and situations, and my impatience all traced back to these underlying fears. Through the power of love, I found a way to weaken the grip of these fear-driven tendencies. As a result, my inner peace flourished, and I embarked on a journey of self-discovery and growth..

****

~ **Diane E***I began my journey with BreathPrayerTM after struggling to overcome my alcoholism through other methods. While I continued attending Alcoholics*

Anonymous meetings and working with my sponsor, I felt compelled to explore a different path. During my first BreathPrayerTM session, I experienced a deep and profound peace that was completely new to me. In my second session, a divine truth revealed itself: much of the fear driving my alcoholism originated from the physical and sexual abuse I had endured from men in my past. In that session, I found the strength to forgive those who had caused me pain and also forgave myself for succumbing to alcohol addiction.

As I dedicated myself to six months of BreathPrayer sessions, I underwent a remarkable transformation. A new, wonderful inner peace took root within me, and I directly attributed this positive change to BreathPrayerTM. Now, when challenges arise in my daily life, I draw upon the profound sense of peace I encountered during my BreathPrayer experience. By doing so, I'm able to regain the inner calm that I had before the problems emerged.

For the first time in my life, I felt like I had a real grasp on my battle with alcoholism and genuine confidence in my ability to fully recover. I also felt a strong urge to share the benefits of BreathPrayerTM with my fellow AA members, so I began promoting its practice among them. This journey has truly been transformative, leading me to a place of healing, empowerment, and newfound hope.

****

~ **Mary F.** *Mary was once an active participant in a thriving residential building business alongside her husband. However, their partnership took a drastic turn when her husband confessed to an affair with a stripper,*

leading to her contracting a venereal disease. To compound matters, he had succumbed to illegal drug use, squandering a staggering $50,000 of the company's funds on drugs and the stripper within a mere two months. This tumultuous revelation prompted Mary to file for divorce, although she was plagued by considerable anxiety about solitude and the potential repercussions on their two children.

During her sessions, Mary experienced a profound emotional release that resonated deeply. Over the span of just a few sessions, she found herself enveloped in an escalating sense of spiritual insight and serenity. Guided by divine truths, Mary embarked on a journey of reconciliation with the inevitability of divorce. She fostered the belief that a benevolent higher power would watch over her and her children during the challenging times ahead.

Within the framework of BreathPrayerTM, a compelling revelation emerged: Mary felt a resounding conviction to engage with troubled teenagers—an idea that had intermittently crossed her mind before. Bolstered by this newfound purpose, she initiated a program through her church, subsequently proving to be a profound blessing for both the young individuals in need and for herself. Presently, Mary finds herself bathed in a sense of divine favor, a sentiment coupled with a more profound peace than she has ever known.

****

Chapter 11: 21-Day Breath of Love Retreat

Welcome to the transformative 21-Day Breath of Love Retreat, a journey that has touched the hearts and spirits of many, unveiling the power of Love Energy within. For some, this practice has been a remarkable catalyst for renewal, prosperity, and profound life changes. Now, it is your turn to embark on this soul-stirring adventure.

i. To begin, prepare a Personal Journal with space for 21 entries, a sacred vessel to hold your reflections and revelations.

ii. Over the next 21 days, immerse yourself in the practice of Breathing Love with circular breaths, dedicating a minimum of 20 minutes each day to this sacred endeavor.

iii. As you breathe in the essence of Truth, let your thoughts flow freely onto the pages of your journal.

iv. Resist the urge to revisit your journal entries for several days or weeks, allowing the seeds of transformation to take root and flourish in the depths of your being.

v.   If, by chance, you miss a day along the way, fear not. Simply start anew with day one (1), for there is a potent spiritual principle at work in *consecutive days* that amplifies the journey's impact.

While it is possible to practice fasting without consecutive days, I have discovered that the results are more potent when you commit to the discipline of 21 consecutive days. The power of consistency enhances the transformative effects of this practice, making it even more profound and rewarding.

With dedication and love, allow this journey to unfold, embracing each day with an open heart and an unwavering commitment. The results that await you are nothing short of extraordinary. Therefore, let the power of Love Energy guide you as you step into the transformative embrace of the 21-Day Breath of Love Retreat. May your spirit soar and your life be forever enriched by this sacred practice. Embrace the journey, for the path of Love leads to wondrous discoveries.

The page was intentionally left blank.

Bibliography

Adler, A. (1950). *The practice and theory of individual psychology (2nd ed.).* London: Routledge & Kegan.

Borysenko, J. (1984). *Minding the body, mending the mind.* New York: Bantam Books.

Brown, R. P., & Gerbarg, P. L. (2005). Sudarshan Kriya Yogic breathing in the treatment of stress, anxiety, and depression. Part II--clinical applications and Guidelines. *Journal of Alternative and complementary medicine (New York, N.Y.),* 11(4), 711–717. https://doi.org/10.1089/acm.2005.11.711

Campbell, J. (1974). *The mythic image.* Princeton, NJ: Princeton University Press.

Campbell, J. (1990). *The hero's journey: The world of Joseph Campbell.* San Francisco, CA: Harper & Row.

Chambers, O. (1962). *Biblical psychology: Christ centered solutions for daily problems.* Grand Rapids, MI: Discovery House.

Daemion, J. (1989). *The healing power of breath: An introduction to holistic breath therapy.* New York: Avery Publishing.

Del Bene, R. (1992). *The breath of life: A simple way to*

pray. **Nashville, TN: Upper Room Books.**

Doll, A., Hölzel, B. K., Bratec, S. M., Boucard, C. C., Xie, X., Wohlschläger, A. M., & Sorg, C. (2016). Mindful attention to breath regulates emotions via increased amygdala–prefrontal cortex connectivity. *NeuroImage, 134,* 305–313. https://doi.org/10.1016/j.neuroimage.2016.03.04 1

Dossey, L. (1989). *Recovering the soul: A scientific and spiritual search.* **New York: Bantam Books.**

Dossey, L. (1993). *Healing words: The Power of prayer and the practice of medicine.* **New York: Harper Collins.**

Eberle, H. (1997). *Spiritual realities: The breath of God in us.* **Yakima, WA: Wine Press.**

Everly, L. (1965). *That man is you.* **Paramus, NJ: Newman Press.**

Fagan, J. & Shepard, I. (Eds.) (1970). *Gestalt therapy now.* **New York: Harper & Row.**

Ferreira, L., Tanaka, K., Santos-GaldURóz, R. F., & Galduróz, J. C. (2015). Respiratory training as a strategy to prevent cognitive decline in aging: a randomized controlled trial. *Clinical interventions in aging, 10,* 593–603. https://doi.org/10.2147/CIA.S79560

Foster, R. (1983). *Meditative prayer.* **Downers Grove, Illinois: Inter-Varsity Press.**

Foster, R. (1992). *Prayer: Finding the heart's true*

home. **New York: Harper Collins.**

Frankel, Y. (1984). *Man's search for meaning: An introduction to logotherapy.* **New York: Simon & Schuster.**

Goldsmith, J. (1959). *The art of spiritual healing.* **New York: Harper Collins.**

Gopichandran, L., Srivastsava, A. K., Vanamail, P., Kanniammal, C., Valli, G., Mahendra, J., & Dhandapani, M. (2021). Effectiveness of Progressive Muscle Relaxation and Deep Breathing Exercise on Pain, Disability, and Sleep Among Patients With Chronic Tension-Type Headache: A Randomized Control Trial. *Holistic Nursing Practice. Advanced online publication.* https://doi.org/10.1097/HNP.0000000000000460

Guyon, J. (1685). *Experiencing the depths of Jesus Christ.* **Sargent, GA: Christian Books.**

Hamasaki H. (2020). Effects of Diaphragmatic Breathing on Health: A Narrative Review. *Medicines (Basel, Switzerland),* 7(10), 65. https://doi.org/10.3390/medicines7100065

Higgins, G. (2019, October 3). Mindfulness can be a powerful conflict-resolution tool. People Management. Retrieved from https://www.peoplemanagement.co.uk/article/1741633/mindfulness-as-a-powerful-conflict-resolution-tool

Holmes, E. (1938). *The science of mind.* **New York:**

Penguin Putnam.

Jampolsky, G. (1979). *Love is letting go of fear.* Berkeley, CA: Celestial Arts.

Jerath, R., Edry, J. W., Barnes, V. A., & Jerath, V. (2015). Physiology of long pranayamic breathing: Neural respiratory elements may provide a mechanism that explains how slow deep breathing shifts the autonomic nervous system. *Medical Hypotheses, 84(2),* 87-90.

Johari, H. (1934). *Breath, mind, and consciousness.* Rochester, VT: Destiny Books.

Kadloubovsky, E. & Palmer, G.E. (1954). *Writings from the Philokalia on prayer of the heart.* London: Faber & Faber.

Kelsey, M. (1972). *Encounter with God.* Minneapolis: Bethany Fellowship.

Kelsey, M. (1976). *The other side of silence: A guide to Christian meditation.* New York: Paulist Press.

Koch, G. (1998). Spiritual empowerment: A metaphor for counseling. *Counseling & Values,* Vol 43, 19-27.

Lampman, C. (1999). *Heart centered breath therapy training.* Seattle, WA: Wellness Press.

Ma, X., Yue, Z. Q., Gong, Z. Q., Zhang, H., Duan, N. Y., Shi, Y. T., Wei, G. X., & Li, Y. F. (2017). The Effect of Diaphragmatic Breathing on Attention, Negative Affect, and Stress in Healthy Adults. *Frontiers in Psychology,* pp. 8, 874.

https://doi.org/10.3389/fpsyg.2017.00874

Marquarrie, J. (1972). *Paths in spirituality*. New York: Harper & Row.

Maslow, A. (1954). *Motivation and personality*. New York: Harper & Row.

McConville, J., McAleer, R., & Hahne, A. (2017). Mindfulness Training for Health Profession Students—The Effect of Mindfulness Training on Psychological Well-Being, Learning and Clinical Performance of Health Professional Students: A Systematic Review of Randomized and Non-randomized Controlled Trials. *EXPLORE, 13(1),* 26-45.

McCullough, M. & Worthington, E. L. (1995). College students perception of a psychologist's treatment of religious issues: Partial replication and extension. *Journal of Counseling & Development:* 73, 636-634.

McLaren, P. (1994). *Life in schools: An introduction to critical pedagogy in the foundation of education (2nd ed.).* New York: Longman.

Morningstar, J. (1994). *Breathing in light and love: Your call to breath and body mastery.* Milwaukee, WI: Morningstar Publishing.

Muller, W. (1992). *Legacy of the heart: The spiritual advantages of a painful childhood.* New York: Simon & Schuster.

Myss, C. (1996). *Anatomy of the spirit: Seven stages of power and healing.* New York: Three Rivers

Press.

Myss, C. (1997). *Why people don't heal and how they can.* **New York: Three Rivers Press.**

Naik, G. S., Gaur, G. S., & Pal, G. K. (2018). Effect of Modified Slow Breathing Exercise on Perceived Stress and Basal Cardiovascular Parameters. *International Journal of Yoga, 11(1),* 53–58. https://doi.org/10.4103/ijoy.IJOY_41_16

O'Hanrahan, P. (n.d.). Conscious Breathing Practices for the Nine Types.

The Enneagram at Work. *Retrieved from* https://theenneagramatwork.com/conscious-breathing-practices

Ornish, D. (1997). *Love and survival: The scientific basis for the healing power of intimacy.* **New York: Harper Collins.**

Peck, S. (1978). *The road less traveled: A new psychology of love, traditional values, and spiritual growth.* **New York: Simon & Schuster.**

Quinn, J. Interview with Dennis Gersten, M.D., "Aids, Hope, and Healing," Part II, *Atlantic: The Imagery Newsletter* (February 1992), 3 ff.

Rossi, E. (1986). *Psychology of mind-body healing: New concepts of therapeutic hypnosis.* **New York: N.W. Norton.**

Rupp, J. (1997). *The cup of our life: A guide of spiritual growth.* **Notre Dame, IN: Ave Maria Press.**

Schucman, H. & Tetford, W. (1975). *A course in miracles.* **New York: Penguin Press.**

Scolastico, R. (1995). *Doorway to the soul: How to have a profound spiritual experience.* **New York: Pocket Books.**

Seamands, D. (1985). *Healing of memories.* **Colorado Springs, CO: Victor Books.**

Seamands, D. (1991). *Healing damaged emotions.* **Colorado Springs, CO: Victor Books.**

Sheehan, P. (1994). *Methods of post traumatic therapy.* **New York: Greenwood Press.**

Smalley, G. & Trent, J. (1988). *The language of love.* **Colorado Springs, Co: Family Publishing.**

Smith, E. (1996). *Beyond tolerable recovery: TheoPhostic counseling.* **Campbellsville, KY: Family Care press.**

Smith, H. (1961). *The world's religions.* **San Francisco, CA: Harper.**

Speads, C. (1978). *Ways to better breathing.* **Rochester, Vermont: Healing Art Press.**

University of Michigan Health. (n.d.). Diaphragmatic Breathing for GI Patients. *Retrieved from* https://www.uofmhealth.org/conditions-treatments/digestive-and-liver-health/diaphragmatic-breathing-gi-patients

Yau, K. K., & Loke, A. Y. (2021). Effects of diaphragmatic deep breathing exercises on prehypertensive or hypertensive adults: A literature review. *Complementary therapies in clinical practice, 43,* 101315. https://doi.org/10.1016/j.ctcp.2021.101315

A Gesture of Thanks

May I express my profound gratitude for your unwavering dedication and courage in delving into the contents of this book. Your willingness to embrace new paradigms of thinking, to wholeheartedly experiment with fresh approaches, and to wholeheartedly experience the profound potency of love energy through conscious breath is both commendable and inspiring.

As you continue on your life's path, my earnest hope is that the boundless reservoir of love within you continues to cast its illuminating light, guiding and blessing each of your days with its radiant presence.

With heartfelt appreciation,

Dr. Scott

Scan the QR code for the website:

www.ingramcontent.com/pod-product-compliance
Lightning Source LLC
Chambersburg PA
CBHW051315120626
46547CB00015B/2251